BEYOND THE
TPS TOOLS

BEYOND THE
TPS TOOLS

PREPARING THE SOIL FOR A LEAN TRANSFORMATION

JON DELONG

Library of Congress Control Number: 2011917060
ISBN: Hardcover   978-1-4653-6398-5
                 Softcover   978-1-4653-6397-8
                 Ebook   978-1-4653-6399-2

This book was printed in the United States of America.

To order additional copies of this book, contact:
Xlibris Corporation
1-888-795-4274
www.Xlibris.com
Orders@Xlibris.com
103648

Table of Contents

The Software—The Human Side Requirements to Sustain TPS

A Time to Reflect—Toyota's Lessons Learned

The Wrap-Up

DEDICATION

First and foremost I thank my Lord and Savior Jesus Christ for giving me the knowledge and the patience to pursue this project. I would also like to say a special thank you to my wife Jolene and to my sons Jake and Josh. I offer my deepest appreciation to Chris, Chad, Sid and Jeff for their valued feedback. Thanks to all of my work colleagues without whom the information in this book would not have been possible. Finally, thank you to the rest of my family and friends for their constant support and encouragement.

JON DELONG

Where to begin? With the basics, I suppose. In June of this year, I turned forty-five, and for the first time since graduating from college, I found myself contemplating my next career move. I currently live in Georgetown, Kentucky, a small town located just a few miles north of Lexington. I spent my childhood and young adult life in Lexington where my parents have lived for almost thirty-five years. This is also where I met my best friend, Jolene, who I married twenty-three years ago. We have two sons, Jacob who is nineteen and attends the University of Louisville where he is studying electrical engineering, and Joshua who is seventeen and is currently a high school senior with dreams of one day becoming a physician or a lead guitarist for a band. One thing for certain, I feel very blessed to have a family that has always loved and supported me.

My formal training is in the field of mechanical engineering. I earned my BSME from the University of Kentucky in 1988. Immediately after graduation, I began working for the Ford Motor Company at their Louisville assembly plant as a facility maintenance mechanical design engineer. I couldn't have asked for a better work experience right out of college. In this role, I not only gained a very broad understanding of facilities equipment and building systems, but I was also able to begin learning the automotive industry from a technical perspective (as opposed to the manufacturing perspective). I felt like this really gave me an advantage later in my career, because many of my peers only knew how to build cars. What they didn't understand was all of the other support systems required to keep the factory running.

As my career progressed, I often reflected back on these first years when I developed a sincere appreciation for the work of engineers in manufacturing. As a mechanical systems designer, I relied heavily on my own engineering education and training, but I also quickly discovered the benefits of being open to learning from others. What amazed me the most (and I often tell my sons this) is that my formal education only partially prepared me for my career. I say this because I received virtually no training on how to interact professionally with other people. Although I loved the engineering work, I found the "people side" of the business to be even more challenging and interesting.

After four years, I was promoted into a management role supervising union skilled tradesmen. Without a doubt, this was the single most educational experience of my life. I found myself working alongside some of the best technicians in manufacturing, and each day was like a classroom experience. Believe me when I say that Ford had some of the most technically capable people in the business. From an engineering and tooling/equipment standpoint, I would say that they were ahead of Toyota at that time. On the other hand, the antagonism of the "union versus company" culture made supervising difficult and unsatisfying to say the least. I spent more time wrapped up in the politics of interpreting a contract than I did in improving operations. It was at this point that I began to struggle with finding balance between my enjoyment of the technical aspects of my job and the constant battles with a complacent workforce. I was beginning to understand that a company's culture can significantly contribute to personal commitment and job satisfaction.

I later went on to some special projects with new model introductions and finally into a role as a superintendent over the largest production area in the plant—general assembly. Now I was not only supervising hourly maintenance workers, but I also experienced the challenge of managing engineers who were my peers. As with most of my work experiences at Ford, I found this job to be very exciting and demanding, but the culture was now taking a toll on me personally. I could feel myself being consumed by the negativity of the work environment. The only priority for the company was to keep cars pumping off the final line. Any time the line stopped, I knew there would be hell to pay from one of the senior managers. By this time nine years had passed, and Jolene and I had started our family. I just couldn't see myself as a future role model for my sons if I remained in this type of work culture. Having only experienced this one culture at Ford, I began to wonder if this manufacturing stuff was the right path for me after all.

In the fall of 1997, I just happened to be in the right place at the right time. My dad was working for Toyota as a contract employee recruiting and assessing skilled team members for their plant in Kentucky. He was hooked up pretty tightly with several of the HR folks there who told him about the hiring activity kicking into full swing at the "new plant" in Princeton, Indiana (commonly known as TMMI—Toyota Motor Manufacturing, Indiana). I was fortunate that TMMI was interested in me, and I was eventually hired as one of the first four employees for TMMI's assembly shop. We immediately began putting together a world-class team to build Toyota's first full-sized truck, the Tundra. I was amazed to see manufacturing from the perspective of Toyota's culture—more widely known as the Toyota Way. I was also surprised to see that Toyota was all about making problems into opportunities versus finding someone to blame.

This initial time with TMMI is also when I began learning TPS (the Toyota Production System). All of my experience with Ford was on the technical support side (engineering and maintenance), so learning manufacturing was completely new to me. I began learning TPS from some of the very best Toyota had to offer. I especially appreciated the guidance of Seizo Okamoto, our president for nearly eight years, and Masahiro Tajiri, our first manufacturing vice president and the current leader of Toyota's global production center. Most importantly, however, these early Japanese *sensei* taught me how valuing people and having the right culture allows TPS to come alive in the workplace. And creating the right culture is exactly what I helped to do as we hired more than 1,700 new employees and successfully launched the Tundra in 1999.

As TMMI continued to expand production operations (eventually to almost 5,000 employees), I advanced my management role until I was ultimately promoted to manufacturing general manager for the entire facility. At this time, we were producing nearly 400,000 vehicles annually with three vehicle types—Sequoia, Tundra, and Sienna. For three years, I was responsible for all manufacturing, engineering, maintenance, and material handling from the press shop through the final assembly area. These years represent my most enjoyable work experience both due to the challenging scope of responsibility and to the breadth of knowledge and skill gained from working with such a talented group of people. As my TPS and Toyota Way skills improved, I became one of the teachers for the rest of the management team. Helping others grow in using these tools was a very fulfilling part of my career.

In 2007, I transferred plants within Toyota to TMMK, Toyota Motor Manufacturing, Kentucky, located in Georgetown, Kentucky. The circumstances I discovered there are actually what inspired me to write this book. TMMK had a rich history and had celebrated many successes including producing the number one selling passenger vehicle in North America, the Camry. This was Toyota's "flagship" plant in North America with over 7,000 employees and had achieved numerous accolades including four JD Power Gold Plant awards. But the "Gold" awards had all dried up, and I soon learned that many of the members of TMMK's management team had become complacent with the status quo. It was difficult to see many of the basic principles of TPS and the Toyota Way being practiced in the plant. I became driven with a desire to bring this culture back to TMMK (or at least the pieces that I managed in the paint and plastics shops), and I found myself sharing many of the lessons I was taught at TMMI. I too became a student while learning how to motivate people by creating a shared vision for success.

By 2011, nearly four years after joining TMMK, I made a tough life decision and left Toyota. Today, I am considering ways to use my knowledge to help others wanting to question the norms within their own organization. Much has been written about TPS and the Toyota Way, but what makes my book different is that I've been a leader at various levels within Toyota personally. I've experienced the full spectrum of Lean cultures—from creating a brand-new culture with a fresh workforce, as I did at TMMI, to leading culture change with an experienced workforce, as I did at TMMK. I don't consider myself to be an author writing a book about how to apply Lean in your workplace. Instead, I'm a manufacturing guy who has devoted himself to TPS and the Toyota Way, and I just happen to be writing a book.

When I'm not preaching TPS, you might just find me riding my Harley ('03 Deuce) or sitting in a tree stand in October with a bow in my hands. I also try to stay very active in my church. About two years ago, I took up playing the drums so I could be in a praise band with my youngest son, Josh. Learning something this mentally and physically challenging has been somewhat frustrating at times, but it's all worth it when we lead our congregation in worship.

So there's my story, or at least part of my life story, I should say. Now this book has literally become the next chapter in my life. I hope that you can look beyond the novice literary aspects of this text and gain some useful insights from my experiences as a Lean leader. Enjoy!

FOREWORD

While there are many books and articles written about the Toyota Production System and the Toyota Way, Jon DeLong's simplified and practical explanation of how Toyota applies these principles is the most accurate. Jon's firsthand experience leading at two of the largest Toyota facilities in North America gives the best unbiased description of the successful leadership styles, methods, and systems that truly make Toyota unique. Jon was directly involved in two major Toyota plant startups, multiple new model introductions, and numerous model changes. He has not only been involved with building the assembly plant from the ground up but more importantly the culture of continuous improvement and respect at TMMI (Toyota Motor Manufacturing, Indiana).

I worked for and with Jon for ten years at TMMI. We learned the Toyota Way by "doing it" on the floor every day. Of course, we had excellent *sensei* to teach and mentor us in the early years. We both have similar backgrounds working at other automotive companies prior to Toyota, and Jon has over twenty years of automotive experience to draw upon. I think the mix of Toyota and non-Toyota experience has been the key to Jon's deeper understanding of many of Toyota's success factors.

I am sure Jon would be the first to admit that he is by no means a TPS/Toyota Way expert. Most of us prefer to think of ourselves as lifelong students. But if there ever was an "expert" on the Toyota Way, I would say that Jon is as close to the title as anyone that I have met. In my ten-plus years at Toyota, I did not meet anyone that had a better grasp of the integrated practical application of the Toyota Way from the floor up to the president. Jon may not have fifty years of Toyota experience or a PhD in management, but he does have one of the best grasps of the overall *practical application* of the Toyota Way, Toyota Production System, and tools on the shop floor.

He has simplified the explanations of the concepts and the reasons behind some of what Toyota does and why. Jon also explains the link between servant leadership and problem solving. If you learn nothing more than the importance of these two things alone, then the time and money spent on this book will be one of the best career investments you ever make. As I mentioned previously, Jon has the unique ability to simplify otherwise complex concepts through analogies and practical life experiences. This is not a book containing lists of guiding principles or complicated leadership models and catch phrases. This is a book that describes how Jon adapted what Toyota taught him and combined it with his life experiences to successfully develop and sustain a culture of respect and continuous improvement.

I have read many of the books written about TPS and "Lean transformation." Jon's book is now at the top of my recommended reading list. I know that readers will have a much better understanding and appreciation of the importance of "preparing the soil" before attempting a Lean initiative at their organization after reading this book. I will use the information and material in this book with my clients and companies as we navigate through the many Lean transformations in the future. I support and encourage Jon to continue writing more works like this for those of us trying to implement Lean on the shop floor and develop a Lean culture at our organizations.

Chris McCoy
Lean Deployment Consultant
CAM Management
and former Production General Manager
Toyota Motor Manufacturing, Indiana

BACKGROUND AND INTRODUCTION

Considering that I am an engineer at heart, constructing this book has been a real labor of love. Those of you who are engineers probably know exactly what I mean. I rarely read books, so believe me when I say that writing one was the furthest thing from my mind. What began as a journaling process to capture my leadership and management knowledge evolved into a more in-depth endeavor. The more I wrote the more I began to realize that others struggling with the complexities of leading and managing in a Lean organization could learn from my experiences. Recently I resigned from a thirteen-year career with Toyota, and a month later I began this project. At the time that I left I was one of only a dozen or so executives holding the production general manager position in North America. The reason for my leaving could possibly be the subject of a book itself, but for the sake of simplicity, let's just say that I left because I had more to offer than I was able to contribute at Toyota.

Toyota has long been known for their manufacturing success and in particular their creation of the management system known as TPS (or the Toyota Production System). Of course, the attraction of TPS to outsiders is based on the premise that the application of TPS principles will eliminate waste and therefore reduce cost. Although Toyota developed these principles decades ago, never before has the thought of reducing waste and controlling cost been more relevant than it is in today's harsh economy. I know this firsthand because I'm in constant contact with companies or recruiters for companies who are aggressively searching for people who can apply these same principles to their businesses.

But studying and attempting to master TPS isn't new. Dozens (maybe even hundreds) of "textbooks" have been written to explain how these tools can be used to highlight and reduce waste in practically any process. This, however, isn't another one of those books. From an instructional perspective, there really isn't anything new that I can add to what has already been written about the "basic" elements of TPS. Conceptually, the tools are not that difficult to understand—at least not from a purely theoretical sense. Here is where the experience that I have acquired begins to come into play. Would it surprise you to hear that even Toyota doesn't apply TPS from a completely theoretical perspective? Perhaps one could argue that nothing is ever executed exactly to plan, but that's not why Toyota deviates from the pure TPS path. The reasons Toyota struggles to follow TPS are the same reasons that many other companies fail to sustain the alluring results that TPS seems to offer—applying TPS principles is not intuitive, it requires great effort to perform, and it often contradicts human nature. The secret to a successful Lean transformation isn't in deployment of the tools, but rather in the creation the right culture.

What is rarely revealed about TPS is that the application of the tools making up this manufacturing philosophy requires very strong discipline and effort to manage. At the same time, the principles are not that difficult to comprehend. One might even say that the tools are nothing more than common sense, but managing using TPS is not easy—especially in the U.S. In Japan, the structured, procedural composition of TPS is more socially accepted, and the Toyota team members there tend to adhere to the rules of these principles more naturally. How do I know this? Because I've observed the production operations of every Toyota plant in Japan, and I've studied the discipline of the workers firsthand. I have also worked in automotive manufacturing in North America for over twenty years, and I can tell you with all confidence that employees in the U.S. are not as willing to work in an environment strictly defined by rules and procedures.

I have several theories for why dissimilarities exist between Japanese and U.S. employees, and I will describe some of these in more detail later in the book. However, if you haven't experienced these cultural and social differences for yourself, then I'm going to ask you to bear with me on this point for a while. The takeaway here is that TPS is not the easiest method for managing a North American business. Honestly, it may be one of the most difficult ways—particularly because our social norms and values tend to be quite different from those in Japan where TPS originated. So it's going to take more effort than simply mastering the TPS tools if you want to successfully implement and sustain Lean in your company. What differentiates Toyota from Ford isn't their tooling, engineering, or even their processes. In many ways, Ford is actually stronger than Toyota in these areas. What makes Toyota unique is how they tap into their people and utilize their capabilities.

Adding to the complexity of any Lean transformation within an existing work culture is a set of conditions I call "organizational equilibrium." What I mean by this is that every organization has become what it is based on a set of circumstances and conditions that exist currently within that environment. These conditions and circumstances include the current management personnel, policies, procedures, cultural norms and practices, the physical environment, each employee's individual behavior, etc. All of these circumstances and conditions combine together to create the organizational equilibrium. When you observe the physical conditions of any organization, you can be assured that everything exists for a reason. If there is excess inventory—it's there for a reason. If there are extra people or processes—they are there for a reason. If processes are not efficient—the inefficiency exists for a reason. If the company is experiencing employee relations issues—these problems exist for a reason. Based on this theory, nothing happens by accident. Everything is occurring according to the natural organizational equilibrium.

Quickly implementing TPS tools without a greater understanding of your company's culture is not a formula for success. Although this is one way to make previously hidden problems visible, the basic rules of TPS will not expose any issues imbedded in the culture of your organization. As with any problem, when the root cause is not thoroughly addressed, the original liability is going to return, because this is how the controlling conditions and circumstances within the organization naturally exist—the organization equilibrium. Companies will often miss the root cause of their issues because their Lean transformation goals focus solely on deployment of the TPS tools versus holistically addressing all of the underlying issues within the deeper organizational equilibrium.

I love to speak in analogies, so here's the best one I can use to illustrate my point. If you've ever tried to lose weight in the past, you know that it can be quite a grueling process. For every person who has tried to lose weight, there are at least two or three people out there who have a plan to help you do it. Some involve diets, pills, or exercise, and there are all sorts of combinations in between. Heck, you can even have some pretty invasive surgery to lose weight if you're willing to make that level of commitment. So which method will most people try first? My experience through the observation of human behavior is that people will choose the solution that is the easiest—the one that requires the least amount of sacrifice. If they believed that simply taking a diet pill would work and no exercise or diet change was necessary, most people would jump all over it! Is this realistic? Can people actually lose weight by simply taking a pill? If so, I'm not aware of this pill. I believe finding the real solution will require a more holistic approach and must address the root cause for the weight gain. The same holistic thinking applies to improving your business conditions. TPS is merely a set of tools—there's absolutely no magic "pill" here.

So what difference does this make? Easy or difficult, how does that change the principles of TPS and what it can offer your business? The answer is that without proper application and the discipline to sustain TPS, no business will ever achieve the desired benefits of reduced costs. There you have it. Successfully implementing a "Lean transformation" isn't about applying the TPS tools, but rather it's about understanding what to do with the waste the tools expose and ultimately sustain the results when the waste is eliminated. Even Toyota struggles with sustaining the results from TPS. The very company that created and tested the principles that others are trying to copy cannot consistently maintain the application of these tools within their own operations. It's not that they don't understand what needs to be done. TPS is well studied and consistently taught in every Toyota plant. Manufacturing using TPS principles isn't a nice idea at Toyota—it's the daily expectation. So why does even Toyota fail to consistently apply TPS? I've found that the problem relates back to people who are either not capable or not willing to consistently execute the strategies with the discipline TPS management requires.

OK, I'm not here to bash Toyota. As I will reveal to you throughout this book, I believe that Toyota is still the benchmark for Lean management in the world. Sure, there are other companies that have made some headway in improving their operations through the implementation of similar tools, but consistently Toyota remains the baseline by which other company's efforts are measured.

What I do want to point out, however, is that Toyota is far from perfect despite a corporate culture that is rooted firmly in the philosophy of this management system. Most other books written about TPS don't highlight this aspect of Toyota. The authors of these books were granted access to Toyota by invitation, and they only observed what Toyota wanted them to see. I've chosen to reveal this side of Toyota because it's from these struggle points that the true learning for other companies can begin.

The more significant and less copied element of Toyota's corporate culture is the real secret to sustaining TPS, and that's the Toyota Way. The Toyota Way describes the values and beliefs that have embodied Toyota since its inception. The soft-side Toyota culture of respecting people and continuous improvement is part of the DNA of the company, and employees are taught the Toyota Way experientially. In other words, they learn by practicing the business methodology firsthand. This would be analogous to asking someone how he learned the values passed down from his parents. There's no formal classroom or curriculum for this type of value based learning, but it happens nonetheless.

The Toyota Way culture built on respecting people and continuous improvement is the soil that allows the TPS seed to grow and survive. Without it or a similar corporate culture, TPS will not be sustainable. The real question is why is managing using TPS principles so difficult to maintain? The explanation of my philosophies and methods to sustain TPS is what this book is about. I was fortunate to have been part of two Toyota plant startups in North America where we created the culture from the ground up. We weren't given a "cookbook" from our Japanese trainers on how this should be done. Instead, we learned by doing—by creating the best company culture where North American workers could successfully follow TPS manufacturing principles. I also worked at Toyota's oldest and most acclaimed assembly plant where I discovered the realities of a stagnant culture where employees were complacent and dissatisfied. On the following pages, I will attempt to pass on my knowledge gained while both creating and transforming cultures within Toyota. Even under the very best of circumstances and working for the company that developed the methodology of TPS, I found the daily management and sustainment of TPS to be quite challenging and at times extremely discouraging.

The information I present in this book is based on the assumption that the reader has only a basic knowledge of Toyota (the company that is) but a fairly good grasp on the tools and philosophies of TPS. I struggled with this arrangement initially because I didn't understand how someone could have a basic knowledge of TPS but not of the company where the system was developed. Over time, however, I have discovered that this is actually the case with most people outside of Toyota. The basic Lean tools all seem to be present and accounted for, but the deeper understanding of how and why these tools were developed is usually missing. This is one of the reasons that I believe other companies may struggle with Lean application in their business. If the core values and beliefs of a company do not align closely with Toyota's, the TPS tools will probably not work (or at least not to the extent that they have worked for Toyota). You may choose to disagree with this viewpoint, and if so, you're probably going to continue to question the content of the remainder of this book. For those of you who are willing to entertain this idea and continue on this journey, you'll find the flow of information through this book as follows:

Core TPS Principles

I cannot begin to discuss any aspect of Toyota or TPS without first establishing a common vocabulary and a basic understanding of the concepts behind the system itself. I'm sure there will be at least some debate regarding several of my definitions and the presentation of the "house" used to illustrate the elements of TPS. After all, there are many different versions of this model and the placement of the various tools. If you find yourself feeling like your technical understanding of TPS differs from mine, I wouldn't get too hung up on it. Within Toyota itself this very same condition exists because most of us learned TPS from other people, not from a textbook. As you will read in greater detail later, Toyota uses experiential types of training versus a more typical classroom style. Learning TPS is a career-long endeavor with skills taught and practiced on the factory floor. The purpose of this chapter is not to teach TPS but instead to create some baseline to introduce the concepts in the rest of the book. Hopefully, you didn't pick this up expecting more information regarding the fundamentals of TPS. I believe the real learning opportunities are in the chapters that follow this general introduction of the system itself.

Key Philosophies Supporting a TPS Culture

These chapters outline several of the underlying company culture elements I find essential to sustaining a Lean transformation of your business. You may have read some of this material in other books, but much of it is based on my own interpretation of Toyota's philosophies combined with several lessons I've learned as a manager and a leader. This combination of hands-on skill acquisition coupled with my years of practical Toyota management will hopefully make the perspective of this text unique from any other. I've been in the manufacturing management profession for most of my career, and some of my personal leadership approach is also woven into these chapters. Admittedly, I'm not an expert in the field of leadership, and I don't profess to be one. There are, however, some very unique effects that organizations will experience when deploying TPS—either when starting from scratch as with a new plant startup or when transforming a current business. As I've already mentioned, TPS is not the easiest way to manage. You will be asking your employees to do things that are not always intuitive—especially if you have managed your operations without TPS in the past. Change of any kind is never easy for an organization to embrace, and the implementation of TPS will almost assuredly meet some resistance from your workforce. Understanding Toyota's key philosophies should serve as a "sanity check" as you question the alignment of all areas of your business to support a Lean transformation.

Although no two people are ever going to think exactly alike, Toyota makes every effort to align the values of their employees with the company. And only those leaders who best exemplify the company's core values (the Toyota Way that is) will continue to advance into the executive ranks. While I was an executive with Toyota, I had the honor of attending the highest level of training and development offered at that time—Toyota's executive development program. A handful of executives from all over the world were selected each year and asked to complete an executive-level problem solving activity. In preparation for this undertaking, we were given an opportunity to meet directly with Toyota's top leaders in order to better understand their perspectives on the philosophies, values, and the overall culture of Toyota. Among these leaders were the present and two former presidents of the Toyota Motor Corporation: Akio Toyoda, Katsuaki Watanabe, and Fujio Cho. I'm not trying to win any bonus points by dropping names here, but what I am trying to establish is a little credibility regarding my understanding of Toyota's philosophies. Some of what I've written was derived from my own application of these teachings in an actual plant environment, but even this personal experience is rooted in the training I received as a Toyota executive.

The foundation of my experiences captured in this book didn't come from reading someone else's autobiography or from an interview. I lived this stuff every day for thirteen years, and I was taught these philosophies by some of the best leaders inside Toyota. Each of the chapters in this section includes some unique perspectives from my personal experiences blended with the Toyota Way. Because I've supplemented many of the Toyota philosophies with my personal leadership values, you will not find all of these principles shared throughout Toyota. I've used some of my own names and descriptions to "bundle" this information the way I used it to manage my teams. You won't find many other people at Toyota referencing the 4As of performance management outside of the folks I used to manage, but the concepts are all embedded in the Toyota Way.

Please pay particular attention to this portion of the book. My intention is not to persuade you to modify your corporate philosophies and values. You don't have to be Toyota to implement Lean strategies, but there are lessons to be learned from the culture where TPS was created. There are significant reasons why Toyota manages the way they do, and as a leader in your organization, I would hope that you could gain some insight from their corporate culture.

The Hardware—How TPS Is Used to Manage

The three chapters found in this next section I refer to as the "hardware" of TPS because the systems described are very tangible and for the most part standardized throughout the company. As such, these systems can be found and readily observed in any Toyota facility around the world. But why would Toyota place so much emphasis on standardizing how the core elements of TPS are used to manage in each of their facilities? The answer is that all of these tools are not meant to be used in stand-alone fashion, but rather they are intended to be used in conjunction with one another. It's the collaborative application of the

TPS principles that creates the management system. Individually, the tools are of little value. Toyota has standardized how these tools are used to ensure that each of their plants is managed similarly.

Once again, the information found in this section may not be new to many people reading this book. If your company has already begun a Lean transformation, then I'm certain there is some structure regarding how these tools are being used as a management system. Or is there? Since leaving Toyota, I have been very surprised to see how other supposed "Lean companies" are applying the TPS tools. It's almost as if implementation of the tool itself is the desired outcome as opposed to applying the tools to actually improve processes and daily operations. One company that I visited recently was very passionate about applying 4S to improve the visual management of their plant. I could see home position markings and labels on virtually every piece of equipment in the building, but there was not one shred of standardized work for any of the processes. My question to one of their managers was, "How can you decide what is needed for your operations (the 'sort' of 4S) without having process standards?" These guys were obviously not trying to improve their processes. Their goal instead was the implementation of the single tool of 4S. Honestly, I don't think they really understood how 4S applied to a complete Lean strategy. However, using this one tool did give the appearance that they were doing "something."

The hardware chapters should help bring some clarity as to how and why Toyota uses TPS to manage. Most notably, this section is kicked off with a chapter on problem solving. Another huge misconception about TPS is that operations will automatically improve when applying it in your workplace. Solely applying TPS, even if it could be executed perfectly, would improve very little in your operations. TPS tools are meant to highlight wasteful conditions in your processes. Once these conditions are made visible, good problem solving must be used to eliminate the waste. But the desired outcome of continuous improvement isn't just about solving problems; it's about solving the right problems. It's about finding those conditions or circumstances that allow waste to live within your organizational equilibrium. As such, there is no more valid reason for managing with TPS than to ensure that the right problems are being identified and then corrected at the root cause.

The Software—The Human Side Requirements to Sustain TPS

The content in this section of the book is filled with many of my own personal leadership values. Unfortunately, the area of human resource management at Toyota isn't as strong as their skill in managing manufacturing. Fortunately for me, I've had mentors outside of Toyota who are great leaders, and they helped me focus my personal development in the areas of leadership and understanding human behaviors. Based on applying these teachings to the Toyota Way values, I was able to develop my own leadership style. Perhaps the ideas shared in this section aren't terribly unique, but they are relevant to leading people. If your company currently has methods for valuing people such as those described in these chapters, then I'd say you're ahead of the game.

My purpose for including these chapters is to accentuate the importance of a company valuing their employees' skill and knowledge. These soft-side skills are extremely important when you manage using TPS because you'll be asking your employees to give so much of themselves to ensure your business is successful. I know I sound like a broken record, but here it is again—managing using TPS is not easy. The discipline required to execute these philosophies goes beyond what many people feel is reasonable. (Recall that I said applying TPS principles isn't always intuitive?) I can tell you this firsthand because numerous Toyota employees have shared their feelings with me on this very issue. What you need to ask yourself is, "How am I going to keep my employees satisfied with their jobs while the details of their work are constantly being scrutinized?" Based on my experiences with new employees and with seasoned veterans, the answer is the same—as a leader, you must be willing to serve your employees. The methods described in this section highlight what has worked for me as I led many diverse groups at all levels within Toyota.

A Time to Reflect—Toyota's Lessons Learned

I wish I could tell you that you'll never experience any problems once you've stabilized your Lean transformation, but that's just not the case. Unfortunately, one of the shortcomings of human nature is that we tend to become complacent when we're successful. The chapter included in this section describes how Toyota fell into some very difficult times despite their commitment to TPS. This was also a time for sincere reflection for me as well. I was a high-level leader within Toyota when these problems occurred, and therefore, I equally shared the responsibility of becoming too complacent. I'm not proud of it, but I have learned from it, and so can you.

One paradox within TPS is that the status quo is continuous improvement. In other words, the normal condition isn't standing still but rather is improving daily. But how do you achieve this in a practical sense? How does management maintain a sense of urgency to improve operations without burning out the workforce? This chapter will describe how Toyota was transforming their daily operations by getting "back to the basics" with their manufacturing. Not only was I part of the breakdown in management that allowed Toyota to get into this situation, but I was also part of the team that developed the plans to pull us back out. My hope is that you will learn from the mistakes that we made and deploy some of these sustainment tools in your initial transformation strategy.

The Wrap-Up

Typically, the final chapter is where everything is pulled together into a neat little package, but in this case, it's not quite that simple. This is a difficult book to read not only because I'm a novice author but also because the details overlap in so many ways. I could have presented this information in almost any sequence because the topics are all woven together. It's like trying to find the beginning of a circle—is there a right answer to where a circle begins? Your guess is as good as anyone else's. So to fully grasp the content of material in this book, you may need to read through it a couple of times. Once you've read the information at the end of the book, perhaps the discussion points at the beginning of the book will be clearer. The concepts all overlap—the hardware is not solely hardware but also partially philosophy and soft-side skills. Similar comparisons could be made for each section of the book.

Well, that's pretty much it for the introduction with the exception of telling one quick story. This story is actually what inspired me to start journaling which ultimately led to creating this book . . .

One afternoon, I was enjoying a beer with one of my friends and former Toyota colleagues. I had just resigned from Toyota a few weeks earlier, and my friend had left about eighteen months prior to that. His new position was heading up Lean initiatives for a large North American manufacturer. He found himself doing a lot of traveling throughout the U.S. to keep up with all of the problems the individual plants were experiencing. This company has a pretty sound background with TPS knowledge, so I was quite surprised to hear that they were still struggling to create the right culture and sustain Lean manufacturing initiatives. I found the realities of the "outside world's" challenges to be quite interesting because I had always assumed that other companies were doing what we were able to do at Toyota.

One topic lead to the next and we eventually began discussing my future career. Of course, the most logical next step for me would be to find another manufacturing company and join their executive team. After all, we both agreed that my Toyota experience was desirable for companies managing using Lean philosophies. Perhaps this career course would be the best fit for me. We also kicked around the idea of consulting, but I must admit this thought made me feel a bit apprehensive. After only a few weeks away from the job, I had already been contacted several times by recruiters and consultants whose clients urgently wanted to get a Lean transformation started. I was left with the impression that these companies all felt that creating a Lean management system could be done by teaching only the basic elements of TPS and facilitating a few kaizen activities. After all, one of the first questions the recruiters always asked was—did I have experience leading kaizen activities and how well did I know the TPS tools? Not once during one of these conversations was the word *culture* ever mentioned.

By beer number two my friend and I were discussing the huge fees that consultants charge and how I could probably earn a pretty comfortable living by supporting just one or two decent sized businesses. There seemed to be no end to the list of companies who wanted to improve by deploying Lean, and they were all interested in the same things—quickly applying the tools of kaizen, 4S, *kanban*, etc. But in the back of my mind, I just couldn't get around the issue of culture. Did any of the guys at these other companies ever try to understand how their culture was going to impact their ability to transform their business using TPS? Knowing what I know, and with a clear conscience, I just couldn't go into a company and begin facilitating kaizen activities without first discussing at length the philosophies and soft-side issues that have made TPS successful at Toyota. For me personally, this is the key to a Lean transformation, not the use of the tools.

After much deliberation and some self-reflection, I felt like journaling my experiences would be the best method for me to organize my thoughts and explain them to someone else. Although I'm all about improving operations, first and foremost I'm about improving people. If my future is in helping others transform their businesses, then I feel I must also include the necessary elements to engage their employees. Not one person ever asked me what I knew about motivating and leading people, but I can tell you that this is where the tires hit the pavement.

So there you have it. I wrote this book to help people willing to learn from my experiences. Regardless of whether you're just getting started, you've tried and stalled, or you're well on your way to transforming your company, I can guarantee that there will be some information here that will help you. Good luck with your journey!

CHAPTER 2

THE TPS BASICS

Chances are good that anyone reading this book is familiar with TPS, so I'm not going to spend a lot of time discussing something that any textbook ever written on the subject can do. My niche isn't in explaining the "textbook" TPS but rather it is in applying practical TPS within your organization. What's the difference? Would it surprise you to know that even at Toyota TPS isn't applied "by the book"? Say it isn't so! Well, this is in fact the case. Some manufacturing sites do a better job than others, but even the plants in Japan do not practice TPS "by the book." During my career at Toyota, I visited every TMC vehicle assembly plant, so I can attest to this firsthand and without any reservations.

Also, please remember that one of the core philosophies of the Toyota Way is the deep-rooted value placed on continuous improvement or kaizen. In other words, if Toyota's plants were perfectly executing TPS, why would the belief in continuous improvement be so deeply imbedded in their Toyota Way culture? Aside from this point, the fact is that Toyota continuously challenges their level of performance and sets higher expectations. So even if they were following "perfect TPS" (if there were such a thing), the drive to push beyond today's performance standards raises Toyota's organization to apply TPS more deeply and more thoroughly each day.

Before we begin discussing the manufacturing basics behind TPS, it's important to understand several other concepts. TPS is a tool to identify problems. As we discussed previously, TPS isn't a problem solving tool as much as it is a problem identification tool. Here is where the "lean" imagery supports the TPS philosophy. When I think of lean I imagine something that is slim, simple, or stripped down. Similar to this lean imagery, when the tools of TPS are implemented properly, processes will be running with the bare bones of resources. What this means operationally is that there is little to no room for error in execution. There's no safety net if something goes wrong. So why would any business want to manage in this way? Wouldn't this cause disruption to operations? Yes it does, and what running lean really does well is highlight immediately where there is weakness in a process. When resources are plentiful the excess covers up the opportunities (i.e., the problems). Adding resources beyond what is necessary may help operationally for the moment, but what most companies have come to realize is that this mode of business cannot be sustained over time. Adding more resources merely masks the problems so they aren't quite as painful—not painful that is until they fester and grow to the point that they become potentially crippling sometime in the future.

Another core principle of TPS is that it can only work successfully in a culture where problems are welcomed, where problems are truly seen as opportunities versus liabilities. In many companies today, the prevalent management style is to treat problems as weaknesses, and all too often, these weaknesses are projected onto some person in the organization. Let's face it; we've all had experiences where we've spent more time figuring out who to blame for a problem than we did trying to solve it. This mindset or culture won't cut it when attempting to implement Toyota's style of TPS. Toyota views problems as a gift—a sign of where future improvements can and should be made. When small problems are addressed quickly and effectively, they will not grow into larger more severe issues. Therein is the gift—large future problems can be avoided when small present issues are identified and corrected.

Here's a chance for you to save some of your valuable time. If you cannot get your arms around the concept that problems are good, then I recommend that you stop reading this book right now. Go play a round of golf or do something else that will create some enjoyment for you, because there will be no further value in continuing with this book if you don't believe that problems can be turned into opportunities. One of the key learning points that I have to offer you is this—TPS is a tool that when used properly will help your company or organization identify problems. This is what TPS does. It won't fix anything—especially if you have no desire to identify the problems hiding within your organization in the first place! This learning point is exactly why I won't spend too much time talking about the basic tools of TPS. Understanding the tools is actually the easy part. As I said earlier, the concepts of TPS are not difficult to comprehend. What is difficult, however, is managing an organization where problems are found daily, and they must be dealt with efficiently and effectively. Don't believe me? Imagine a facility that is using TPS tools to identify problems but nothing is being done to address them. Have you ever seen the movie *Groundhog Day*? Well that's what you'll turn your workforce into if you're not careful. Nothing will destroy an organization quicker than facing the same problems every day and doing nothing to correct them.

So if for no other reason than to achieve a common vocabulary, here's a simple explanation of the basic TPS components. The visual model used within Toyota depicts TPS as a house (see figure 2.1 below).

Figure 2.1   **The TPS "House"**

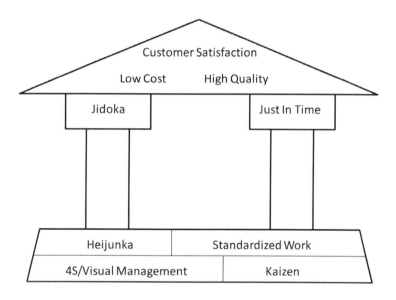

This visual representation emphasizes the key elements of the system as a structure; the foundation, the pillars, and the roof. There are many different versions of this model, but here, I am using what I believe to be the most basic version with the essential elements. Conceptually, TPS is not complicated, so overstating the model would be counterintuitive. From a TPS perspective, basic and simple is good.

The Foundation

Anyone with construction experience understands that regardless of what type of structure you are building, the final product will only be as sound as the foundation on which it is built. Because the foundation is so critical for a strong building, we will begin our basic TPS discussion with the foundation and work our way up through the "house." The key elements of the foundation (those commonly included by Toyota) are; 4S/visual management, *heijunka*, kaizen, and standardized work. These four elements make up the basic concepts to understanding and applying the rest of the TPS tools. Just as a house will not stand without a firm foundation, the application of TPS without a firm understanding of these four principles will be weak and unstable.

4S and Visual Management—One of the most basic foundation blocks within TPS is 4S. (Or is it 5S? The answer is that the original Toyota TPS references only 4S's. The fifth S—sustain—has been added to emphasize the continuous improvement element of TPS.) So what are the 4S's and what do they mean? The 4S's stand for (in very loose translation from the original Japanese version) sort, straighten, sweep, and standardize. Sometimes, shine is used in place of sweep, but in general, these are the accepted, translated 4S meanings. The practical applications of the 4S's are as follows:

- *Sort*—Segregate what is needed to support your process from what is not needed. Anything that is excess in the process is a risk for hiding a potential problem.
- *Straighten*—Everything that is left in the process will require a defined location or home position. The best home position should be established by applying good principles of ergonomics, safety, quality, and productivity. The purpose of the home position is to simplify locating what is needed.
- *Sweep*—The area within the process must be kept clean in order to maintain a safe work environment and to accommodate quick identification of any abnormal sources of contamination (for example: leaking equipment, spilled material, roof leak, etc.).
- *Standardize*—Once the necessary equipment is in a home position and the area is clean, the layout should be standardized by using floor markings, shadow boards, etc. Visualizing the standard condition will

ensure that anything out of place or missing is accounted for quickly and with minimal effort.

The overall objective for 4S is to create a high level of visual management within each process. The visualization is not necessarily intended to assist the person working within the process, but instead, the purpose is to make identification of abnormality simpler for those whose role it is to observe the process. Visual management of what's needed for the process is typically not necessary for the operator who performs the work. The general assumption is that the people performing the process have some proficiency in what they are doing, and they already have a pretty good idea regarding what is needed. If anything, the tendency of the operator is to hoard resources within the process and create waste in the form of excess. Having only what is needed visualized within the process makes confirmation of the production conditions quite simple for the observer—say for the supervisor or for another support resource. Simple, efficient confirmation of process conditions is important because this allows for more time to be devoted to solving the problems that are identified.

Heijunka—In keeping with the theme that basic and simple is good, the most basic and simple definition of heijunka is "smooth and level." In the context of TPS, heijunka refers to the method of leveling or smoothing production so that workers can perform standard tasks without disruption to their process due to peaks or gaps. Regular patterned production also promotes a material delivery system that can be smooth and continuous with a minimum of required inventory. As with almost every element of the TPS model, there are going to be exceptions and/or different levels of adherence. The level of acceptable production fluctuation must be determined by the end user. There is no magic formula that determines how much fluctuation is permissible. In the strictest application of TPS, however, the heijunka should be smooth with minimal fluctuation. Any gap from the ideal condition should be recognized as an opportunity for improvement, and some kaizen activity should be initiated immediately. Fluctuations in the process will most likely lead to one of the following conditions:

1. Inefficient standardized work that accommodates varying job content by adding processing time.
2. Operators will deviate from their standardized work because the fluctuations create production patterns of varying work content.

Neither of these outcomes is desirable, and the process fluctuations should be quickly reduced or eliminated if possible.

Kaizen—An acceptable translation or definition of kaizen is continuous improvement. Continuous improvement comes in all shapes, forms, and fashions. There are two consistent misconceptions that I have observed regarding kaizen. The first is the notion that kaizen is an innovative, quantum-leap type of improvement, and the second is that kaizens are always successful. With regard to the notion that kaizen is innovative, I must say that some of the best examples of kaizen that I have seen have been some of the most simple. The ideas for the kaizen did not come from engineers or PhD candidates, but rather the ideas came from the people directly involved in the process itself. The true concept of kaizen stems from the premise that each person performing the work should have the best experience to draw from when considering how a process can be improved. After all, in the repetitive motion world of assembly line manufacturing, aren't the "assemblers" the folks that have the most familiarity with the work being performed? Additionally, kaizen creates ownership of the process by the members performing the work. Ownership and engagement of the shop floor work is essential in successfully implementing TPS. Kaizen without ownership at the floor level will not be sustainable regardless of how ingenious the ideas seem.

As for the second point regarding kaizen success versus failure, I will simply say that as with most of life's lessons, we tend to learn more from our failures than we do from our successes. Now that doesn't mean that I would encourage anyone to haphazardly start changing elements of a process simply for the sake of change. Any improvement should be thought out and justified with some predetermined performance improvement as a target. In other words, process changes should be made with intentionality—with a purpose in mind. The results of the kaizen should be observable and therefore measurable, and at the end of the day, the improvement should have some positive impact on operations.

At the same time, however, some organizations tend to get change atrophy or analysis paralysis when it comes to kaizen. Any type of change takes some courage to overcome risk. Not every possible outcome can be rationalized by data. Effective kaizen requires a culture of creativity and trust—trust that mistakes will be embraced as opportunities and not a reason to fear punishment. This holds true for the implementation of TPS as a whole. People must be involved at all levels. People are going to make mistakes. People will not engage if they believe problems or mistakes will result in some punitive reaction from top management.

Standardized Work—Standardized work is the glue that holds TPS together. It defines the process in written and visual form. Without documentation of the standardized work for use as a reference, there is no standardized work. The fact that the work is documented is what makes it the standard—the common method or one single way that the process is to be performed. Another way of looking at standardized work is that it's the "plan" for how the work is to be executed. Built into this plan are the very best methods to achieve a balance between good safety, quality, and cost. By creating a holistic strategy for the work method, we can be assured of repeatable, acceptable results. The standardized work also serves as the one and only tool used to train all members who will be performing that particular process. Consistency in the work method will help to eliminate fluctuation and variation within the process. Finally, standardized work establishes the baseline by which all kaizen can begin. Without having some process baseline, improvement would be impossible. Each time the process is improved through kaizen, a new standard is established, documented, and taught to the employees performing the work. The new standardized work then becomes the baseline for the next kaizen—thus creating the cycle of continuous improvement and standardization illustrated in figure 2.2.

Figure 2.2   **The Cycle of Continuous Improvement**
                    and Standardization

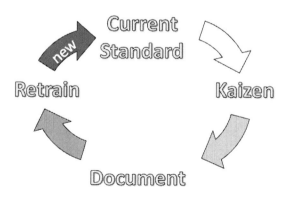

Here is one last thought about standardized work that will be discussed in more detail in chapter 8—"The Process of Problem Solving." The standardized work or method is only one of four key elements (or the 4Ms) that make up the complete process. The other elements are material, machine, and man (or the employee himself). When creating the standardized work, a good rule of thumb is to develop a method that is "easier to do right than it is to do wrong." Complexity in the standardized work generally adds no value to the finished goods once a process has been completed. A person who can be confident and successful in completing the standardized work, however, adds infinite value to the final product—and after all, isn't the final product what the customer is paying for? Does the customer recognize any value in the completed product based on how difficult the work method was? The complete process should maximize the capability of the person performing the work by balancing the man (person's skills), the method (the standardized work), the material (component parts, subassemblies, raw materials, etc.), and the machine (all tools used to assist the assembler). If all of the burden of the process is put on the man due to imbalance in the other three elements, the employee is going to be overwhelmed, frustrated, and more than likely unsuccessful.

The rest of the foundation of the TPS house varies from model to model, but these are the basic elements. Remember, this isn't a model representing your business or your organization. If it was you might want to include things like your company's values in the foundation. I think it's terrific if you're thinking in these terms, but Toyota incorporated the values of the company in another core document called the Toyota Way. The TPS "house" model only includes the basic elements of the manufacturing philosophy.

The Pillars

It's doubtful that any TPS house diagram you find will have more than two pillars. Those two pillars are JIT (just in time) and *jidoka*. Any model with more than two pillars is a representation of someone else's image of TPS, and it does not reflect Toyota's teachings. The pillars make up the core manufacturing philosophy of Toyota which can only be implemented once a sound foundation is in place. Execution of the JIT and jidoka manufacturing methods is not possible without already establishing 4S, heijunka, standardized work, and a process for kaizen. As we discuss these two manufacturing methods, you might also detect that there is a bit of a paradox surrounding the TPS philosophy. This contradiction does not exist in the pure sense of TPS, but practically speaking, it cannot be avoided.

JIT—This philosophy can be summarized by the following conditions: having all the required production resources, in the correct amount, and at the time when they are needed. JIT refers to all elements and/or resources of the process, not just to the material as many people assume. JIT is about having just the right amount of everything—not too much and not too little. You may be thinking that having too little of something is easy to understand as a problem, but why is having too much a problem? The most prevalent answer is that having too much of something translates into excess cost. Yes, this is true from a "onetime cost" standpoint of eliminating unnecessary inventory, equipment, manpower, etc. However, the more important reason to eliminate excess is that it hides other waste within the process. For example, if there is already too much inventory in a process, how can part-flow shortages into a process be easily recognized? The problem created by reduced flow into the process will be hidden by the excessive inventory already on hand, but when inventory is kept at required levels, material flow issues can be detected right away.

There are many other examples of why excess resources can be detrimental. What if more equipment capacity exists than is required based on current demand? Vital equipment downtime and productivity issues could be hidden and go unresolved (until that extra capacity is actually required and not available that is). Or there may be more maintenance people supporting the equipment than what is needed, but how can this be visualized when the excess equipment is in service? Perhaps the excess equipment capacity is causing a buildup of WIP (work in process) while the preceding process is lagging behind? Unless the extra WIP is removed, the imbalance in production rates will be hidden. In a society where excess is generally desirable, convincing a workforce to maintain minimum levels of inventory is very challenging but necessary if TPS is to be implemented fully.

Takt time is a term used in conjunction with JIT to define the speed or rate of production required to meet the customer's demand. Remember that JIT means producing what is needed when it's required—right? Well why would you produce something that has no customer? Isn't the most expensive inventory the inventory of finished goods? Finished goods represent the maximum investment of time, effort, and cost, so having them sitting around collecting dust can be very expensive. Also, finished goods will need to be carefully stored (another cost), ideally in a manner where they retain their full value. Production based on a takt time eliminates the waste of creating finished goods inventory and the risk of lost profits due to unwanted or damaged products. Does this mean there is no finished goods inventory at Toyota? Not quite, but the ideal condition would be zero or near-zero finished goods inventory.

In order to build by takt time, a producing frequency must be developed based on the customer's demand for the products being made. In doing so, the business/industry type must be considered and market conditions anticipated for both short-term and long-term production requirements. Based on the short-term forecast, the processes will be set up at the speed or pace which supports the customer's "pull" or demand. At Toyota, this process occurs monthly. The long-term forecast should be used to study the producing capacity of your processes. When capacity is insufficient to support the long range forecast, consideration should be made for expanding the output of "bottleneck" processes. The key to takt time is this—the rate of production should be based on the customer's demand, not on the producing capability of the processes. Capacity in excess of the customer demand should be idled to reduce costs and expose hidden waste in the processes.

Jidoka—The second pillar of TPS is jidoka. Simply stated, Jidoka means to prevent passing on a defect. Sakichi Toyoda, the founder of Toyoda Automatic Loom Works Ltd. and the father of Kiichiro Toyoda, the founder of Toyota Motor Corporation, is credited with pioneering this concept when he designed a feature into one of his fabric looms. The loom would automatically pause if a broken thread was detected. Thus, the loom was designed to stop producing if a defect was encountered. The significance of jidoka is that process standardization cannot exist if defects are allowed to pass between processes (i.e., there is no standard for a defect—defects are abnormal). The paradox of TPS mentioned previously is that JIT cannot exist between processes when any one process stops because abnormality is detected. So JIT can only truly exist when there are no abnormal conditions? Basically yes, but again we may be splitting hairs here. The emphasis of TPS is on producing at the right time and in the right quantity, but the products being produced must meet the standards and the expectations of the customer. Producing goods that are not at the desired quality level is purely a waste of time and effort.

There are several methods used within Toyota to prevent defects or nonstandard conditions from being passed between processes, but the two most prevalent are the *poka-yoke* and the *andon*. A poka-yoke (sometimes called a "foolproof") is a device or a mechanism whereby a nonstandard condition can be detected without human judgment. The earlier discussion of Sakichi Toyoda's loom is a great example of a poka-yoke. The machine itself was equipped with a device that could detect a loss of tension in a thread and therefore automatically stop the loom. The operator of the loom did nothing other than replace or repair the problem once it was detected by the machine. A modern form of equipment poka-yoke includes mechanical fastener tightening tools that automatically measure torque and have interlocks to conveyors to prevent part flow between processes when specified torques are not achieved. Some poka-yoke characteristics are built into materials or parts themselves. For example, a part which can only be installed in a single direction due to its natural geometry is a type of poka-yoke because the assembler has no option regarding the part's configuration—only one way is correct. The key point here is that defects are nonstandard and that allowing defects to flow from one process to another will start a chain reaction of nonstandard conditions. The poka-yoke simplifies the process for the operator and reduces the likelihood of defects being produced (note: most poka-yoke devices are not completely "foolproof").

The second commonly used method of jidoka is the andon. The andon is a system designed to be used by the operator within a process to stop the process's progression when abnormality is detected. The type of system used for an andon can vary widely, but regardless of how the system is designed, the purpose for the andon is to give control of the workflow to the person or the people working within the process. This too can be a point of contention for many companies. Relinquishing control of the production rate to those within the process can be a pretty scary concept. After all, what happens if people just want to shut the process down so they can take a break? What if people are upset about something and they want to "get back" at management?

If these types of concerns exist within your company, then I can assure you that there are bigger problems than the andon system! There might be other trust issues going on and perhaps some communication difficulties with employees, but the addition of an andon system won't be the root cause of the problem. Actually, adding an andon system might be a step in the right direction toward mitigating some employee issues. Giving workers a means to control the progress of their process exhibits trust from management and empowers employees to take ownership. More importantly, the andon is the system by which an employee can raise a problem up to management so it can be remedied.

Let's go back a few steps. If the "foundation" portion of TPS is already in place (which it should be if systems for JIT and jidoka are being considered), then standardized work should already exist for every process. So what happens when an employee cannot follow standardized work? What happens when a condition outside of the normal process occurs, i.e., a tool breaks or an operator makes a defect or a mistake of some kind? The jidoka concept can no longer be followed if the employee who recognizes a problem continues to produce, because he will be passing something to the proceeding process that is not standard. When this happens, the andon is the tool that workers should use to stop the process and "register" a problem occurrence with management.

The responsibility of management then becomes removing the abnormal condition from the process so the employee can continue performing standardized work. Allowing nonstandard conditions to persist in a process, especially after an employee has identified the condition by use of the andon, creates many undesirable issues. One significant consequence is that the employees will stop using the andon and management will become unaware of the now "hidden" problems within their processes. Management will also lose integrity with their workforce, because although they have given the employees the tools necessary to follow TPS principles, the management team itself does not have the discipline to manage accordingly. Finally and most importantly, once employees feel that they can no longer elevate problems to their management, they will lose engagement. Regardless of how talented and capable a management team might be, TPS cannot work within an organization when all employees are not engaged.

The Roof

Finally, we must discuss the roof of the house. When we think of a roof, we generally think about what protects us from the elements—the rain, the snow, etc. In other words, the foundation and the structure of the house are holding up what protects us from the outside environment. The roof is what shields us from danger and gives us shelter. Well, in a way, the roof of the TPS model is very similar. The TPS roof consists of what Toyota (and any company following TPS) is trying to achieve—the mission and goals if you will. Of course, every company may have a different mission, but some of the common elements probably include; satisfied customers, great quality, and low cost. Within Toyota, short lead time (or delivery time) to the customer is one measurement of customer satisfaction, and this goal is generally shown within the roof of the house as well.

Customer Satisfaction—Let's start with customer satisfaction. It sounds like common sense really, and it would stand to reason that any company that wants to have longevity in their respective market would be interested in happy customers. Specifically within Toyota, the goal of customer satisfaction consists of several elements other than just happiness. First, within the Toyota philosophy, the term *customer* would refer to any person, organization, or community that is a stakeholder with Toyota. This would include not only the person who is buying a Toyota product, but it would also include suppliers, dealers, local communities where Toyota does business, stockholders, employees, etc. Again, anyone who has equity in Toyota is a customer in a broader sense. So customer satisfaction could mean more than someone who is happy with his vehicle. To a stockholder for example, customer satisfaction might be a nice dividend check or a healthy return on an investment. For someone living in a community where Toyota does business, customer satisfaction might take the form of philanthropy efforts or good environmental achievements. The point is that TPS should be applied holistically to support a broad range of customers and stakeholders. For Toyota to fully benefit from TPS, all stakeholders must benefit. When any one of these stakeholders is not satisfied, the longevity of the company is at risk (but we'll discuss this concept in more detail in the next chapter).

High Quality—The second element of the roof is high quality. Why is great quality important to Toyota? Again, the answer seems obvious, but it's actually not quite as simple as it may seem. When Toyota first introduced their vehicles in the United States in the late 1950s, the reputation of the company was not so great. During this time, there was (and perhaps there still is) quite a sense of nationalism in the U.S., and Toyota was seen as a "foreigner." All Toyota brand vehicles during this time were being imported from Japan, and that didn't appeal to many people in the U.S. who wanted to support the domestic automotive companies. Another reason that Toyota struggled initially was that the quality of their vehicles was perceived to be inferior to that of the U.S. car companies (I say "perceived" because quality is defined differently by everyone). To improve sales in the U.S. market, Toyota needed to stand out, and over time, quality became the main differentiator for Toyota products. This didn't happen overnight, but by the early 1980s Toyota products were consistently being recognized within the automotive industry as having "high quality." Some customers were purchasing Toyota vehicles solely for what they believed to be superior quality over the rest of the car manufacturers. It became Toyota's niche. One could argue that today this quality edge no longer exists between Toyota vehicles and their competition, but for the purposes of understanding the TPS house, it is important to understand why quality was included as part of the roof. Quality represented Toyota's excellence—what set Toyota apart from their competition and created the appeal for their customers. For every company this "excellence factor" may be different, but whatever it is, it belongs in the TPS model roof.

Low Cost—Low cost is the final element of the TPS house roof. Many people wonder why this element emphasizes cost instead of profitability—a reasonable question, I might add. The answer is a matter of basic math actually, but first some historical reference is required. Toyota began as a company with very meager financial resources. To say that Toyota was frugal would be a major understatement. Additionally, Toyota has always considered that first and foremost, they are a manufacturing company—in other words, although there are many facets of the company's business including sales, finance, research and development, etc., Toyota's "core business" is manufacturing. With their roots in manufacturing and a history of meager financial resources, Toyota began to look at profitability from a different vantage point than other companies of the day. For many companies, profit is a target in and of itself. Stated differently, the profit was a fixed value. The following equation will help visualize this thinking:

$$\text{Sales Price} = \text{Profit} + \text{Cost}$$

Applying this thinking, the sales price would be set by a company based on covering their costs and the amount of profit they had targeted. Although mathematically the factors are the same, Toyota's business approach toward profitability is much different. They believed that the market conditions and the customer would control the sales price and that the only true factor that could be controlled within the company was cost. As such, the only way to assure a profit from the manufacturing standpoint was to control cost. This thinking can best be visualized as follows:

$$\text{Profit} = \text{Sales Price} - \text{Cost}$$

So mathematically these two equations are exactly the same, but philosophically the difference in thinking is huge. In the first example, the assumption is that the sales price can be set by the company, thus ensuring that a level of profitability is achieved. When using this type of thinking, there tends to be very little emphasis on cost. In order to make more profit, the sales price could simply be increased.

The Toyota model has a completely different focus. Here the assumption is that cost is the only factor that can be controlled directly by the company. As such, profit is the outcome of subtracting the controlled cost from the sales price that is naturally set by the market. So because profitability is achieved by controlling cost, Toyota emphasizes low cost as one of the key objectives within the roof of the TPS house.

So now we have discussed many of the basic elements of TPS. Honestly, there are much better summaries of the TPS principles and philosophies in print if that's what really peaks your interest. Again, however, the purpose of this book is not to explain the Toyota Production System. My intention is to describe how my own experiences in practically applying these principles over the past thirteen years within a North American Toyota facility have helped me effectively manage an organization. Understanding the philosophy of textbook TPS and applying TPS practically in the workplace are two completely different subjects. For the remainder of this book, I will be referring back to many of these basic TPS principles and add insights as to how they can be applied practically and with success within your company. However, the main takeaway will be in understanding how working within these TPS principles and the values of the Toyota Way can positively impact you as a person, as a manager, and especially as a leader.

CHAPTER 3

KNOWING AND UNDERSTANDING YOUR STAKEHOLDERS

Have you ever taken the time to consider who the stakeholders are in your company—Customers? Stockholders? Suppliers? Local communities? Employees and their families? The environment? Any or all of these might depend on your company in some way. Knowing and understanding your stakeholders are two of the most important pieces of information you will need when deploying TPS and the Toyota Way approach in your business. Why? Because TPS and the Toyota Way are simply tools to help achieve a means to an end. When these tools aren't used for their intended purpose, they are ineffective. For example, would you use a saw to drive a nail into a board? I guess you could if you wanted to pound the nail in using the handle of the saw, but wouldn't a hammer work better? Maybe a more important question is, "Even when you know how to use a hammer and a saw for their intended purposes, does that make you a carpenter?" The carpenter in this analogy is the person or the company that can fully deploy the tools of TPS and the Toyota Way. Partially applying some of the tools randomly is a formula for frustration and for mixed results at best, but this is what I believe many companies are doing today.

Knowing the vocabulary of TPS and how to apply it to certain scenarios in your business does not make you capable of leading a Lean transformation. Remember, you picked up this book for a reason, and I believe that reason is to gain a better understanding of how Toyota has achieved their remarkable performance over the past three or four decades. In this chapter, we're going to briefly discuss the "why" of TPS and the Toyota Way. I believe this to be critically important for anyone considering a Lean transformation. You should

30

already have some image of what achievement looks like for your business, and just maybe TPS isn't really the right tool for the job. Even when you are familiar with the concepts, implementation of TPS in and of itself shouldn't be the final, desired outcome. I've included this chapter on Knowing and Understanding Your Stakeholders to offer an explanation of how and why TPS was born inside of Toyota, if for no other reason than to make sure that you're using the right tool for the right job.

When Toyota began operations in 1937, the company had few financial resources and their technical capability for automobile manufacturing was being developed on the fly. But why did Kiichiro Toyoda take on this challenge—a challenge that most rationally thinking people would have avoided at all costs? Was he a capitalist interested in making a quick buck (or yen)? Was he an inventor looking for the next market for his latest gadget? Not even close. Yes, Kiichiro did come from a family of technical accomplishment, but their expertise was in building looms, not in the automotive industry. And although the Toyoda family was by no means poor, they were not a family of wealth either. So why would someone with modest resources and skills want to risk everything that he had on a dream of starting a car company? The answer is not intuitive by today's standards. Simply stated, Kiichiro Toyoda started Toyota Motor Company Ltd. not because he wanted to make cars, but because he wanted to make a difference.

For Mr. Toyoda, the dream was to create a national icon that could be a stepping stone for Japan's industrial expansion into new world markets. He wanted to create jobs and purpose for people living in Japan—not just jobs for Toyota employees, but also jobs for suppliers and for local businesses that would support Toyota's operations. He wanted to create a product that would bring value and great benefit to the people of Japan. Kiichiro understood that business should have a customer-first attitude and that strong corporate citizenship was paramount to any meaningful corporate culture. Mr. Toyoda didn't have all of the answers when he started the Toyota Motor Corporation, and he certainly didn't have the tools of TPS. What he did have, however, was a keen image of who his stakeholders were and how he envisioned his company's purpose for them.

Is this so important? That was then and this is now. He was starting a car company in 1937 and your business is completely unrelated and relevant to a different place and time—right? Yes, you're right, but that's not the point that I would like to make. The point is that regardless of what your company produces or what service it provides, there are stakeholders out there depending on your business to be successful—successful financially, morally, ethically, socially, environmentally, etc. The culture within Toyota that created TPS and the Toyota Way was not solely focused on profitability. I would say that my experience with Toyota would support quite the opposite thinking actually. The Toyota that I know is socially and morally conscious first, ethically rooted in its business practices, and considerate of customer loyalty and satisfaction over dividends to stockholders. Don't get me wrong, Toyota doesn't exist in a fairy tale where everyone is walking around holding hands and singing 1960s flower songs, but the bottom line at Toyota isn't just the financial bottom line—it's much, much more.

If you're still not convinced, then you may be looking for a tool other than TPS. As discussed in the introduction, I believe that there are many misconceptions regarding TPS and how it has been used to make Toyota a leader in manufacturing. Lean (as in scarce) does not equal TPS, but many people believe that it does. Six Sigma does not equal TPS. Right or wrong, the tools of Six Sigma are not practiced at Toyota. If you want a company that runs on bare essentials and uses SPC (statistical process control) as a capability tool to identify process risks, then go for it. Just don't think for a minute that what you are doing even remotely resembles what Toyota is doing with TPS.

My message is simple and unshakable—there is no TPS manufacturing philosophy without first being born from the Toyota culture—the Toyota Way if you will. This is why most companies who have tried to copy TPS principles in the past have not realized the same benefits as Toyota. It's like trying to transplant polar bears into the rainforest. There's a reason why polar bears don't live in the rainforest, and you cannot simply will them into existence there. Companies that already have strong cultures may not be the right environment for emulating the Toyota Way. My opinion on this topic is that the companies having the best chance to implement TPS are those that closely match the conditions in which Toyota began their own business—in other words small, family-owned and operated companies with strong values for services and social responsibility. Larger companies with long established business practices and strongly defined corporate cultures would most likely not want to assimilate to Toyota's culture, and I don't blame them. These companies have spent years building their business based on a separate culture and vision, and they should be proud of that. In the analogy of the polar bear, these companies have a rainforest environment which is fine, unless you're a polar bear.

Still interested in TPS? If so, take a few minutes to thoughtfully consider who your company's true stakeholders really are. Some will be easier to identify than others, but essentially the question you need to ask is, "Who is depending on us to be successful and how do we define success?" We'll talk about defining success in the next chapter as this is equally important to understanding your stakeholders. However, my belief is that you cannot understand what success looks like until you understand first who your stakeholders are. This was the approach taken by Kiichiro Toyoda. He started with the vision of "who" his company would support and "what" he wanted his company to represent. He worked on the part of "how" to achieve these results after creating this vision.

Once you've jotted down who your stakeholders actually are, you may begin to see that you've come up with quite a diverse list. Some names on the list may represent groups of people (employees, stockholders, local legislators, customers), other names may represent organizations outside of your own (local governments, suppliers, service providers), and still other names may represent broader, more abstract entities (the environment, technical or educational systems, etc.). The possibilities are endless, and the list you come up with is most likely going to be very specific to your company. For that reason, it's virtually impossible for me to do anything but speculate about the range of diverse stakeholders your company might have. Nonetheless, I am convinced that the names on your list will be diverse not only in their roles but also in their expectations.

Consider for a minute how varied your business decisions must be in order to support such a broad diversity of stakeholders. Some stakeholders will be primarily concerned with your business's financial stability and growth potential. These individuals are in it for the money, and anything that isn't putting coin in their pocket is wasteful and should be eliminated. Other stakeholders will want corporate citizenship to be the main priority, and the emphasis of these entities will be on how your company supports local communities through philanthropy and service projects. Sure, civic groups want your company to be profitable, but to the extent that you use your profitability to benefit the community where you do business. Customers will want to see investment in technology and improvements in quality that bring more value to the products and services they are purchasing. Customers who are not invested in your company or living in your local community generally could care less about your dividends and your philanthropy. They desire quality, competitiveness for products and services, and value.

Sounds like a lot of work. For what possible reason would anyone want all of these stakeholders? It would be much simpler to just have one or two that "really matter" and ignore the rest. After all, it's difficult enough to make decisions that please a handful of people let alone a large, diverse group like this. I must admit that I never really understood the answer to this question until about two years ago when Toyota fell under scrutiny for the "unintended acceleration" issues with their vehicles. I'm not going to discuss what was going on with vehicles and claims from some owners at this time, but what I will tell you is that it was Toyota's stakeholders that helped pull them through this issue. Loyal communities, customers, legislators, people from the private sector running charitable organizations, employees and their families all backed Toyota. I'm convinced that without this loyalty and support, Toyota on their own would not have survived. Sure, they wouldn't have gone bankrupt or anything like that, but in my opinion, their reputation would have been ruined, and their future share of the automotive market in the U.S. would have been slowly reduced to the point of no return.

Balance is key and that's exactly what TPS and Toyota Way management can bring to your organization. Business decisions must be made and priorities must be set holistically with all stakeholders in mind. For example, perhaps one of your suppliers is struggling and causing you to miss some shipments which is adding cost to your operations. The logical thing to do would be to cut your losses and find another supplier—right? Perhaps, but isn't this supplier one of your stakeholders? Don't you have some vested interest in their success? Isn't the relationship between supplier and customer symbiotic in principle? There's a cost to staying with this supplier that is struggling, but what you've got to realize is that there's also a cost to letting them go. First and foremost, you'll destroy a relationship with a stakeholder which is something you will probably never recover. Second, you're going to need to replace the supplier with someone else which is going to involve time and expense. Finally, you're sending a message to your other stakeholders that if they can't "cut it," they'll be the next ones you cut loose. This isn't the way you build advocates and partnerships that help you through difficult times. Cutting the supplier loose is a shortsighted approach versus investing in the supplier and helping them resolve their issues. This latter option will create partnerships, alliances, and loyalty that will benefit both parties long term.

Much of this chapter has been more about the Toyota Way than TPS, but there is application to stakeholders in TPS as well. Within Toyota's manufacturing, there are five main missions—safety, quality, cost, productivity, and employee development. Each of these missions supports different stakeholders, but for Toyota, they are all equally important to their operation. Each mission may have a different priority depending on the nature of business conditions at any given time, but all five are significant and require constant attention and resources. At no time would one mission be completely sacrificed for the achievement or the advancement of another. TPS and good problem solving are the tools Toyota uses to ensure a balanced approach within manufacturing that sustains all stakeholders. Visually, this manufacturing philosophy looks like a five axis scale being balanced by the five missions (refer to figure 3.1). Within this metaphorical balancing act, as priorities change, the axis becomes shorter and more effort (or in the case of a scale, more "weight") must be applied to keep everything balanced.

Figure 3.1   **Five Missions Are Balanced to
Sustain all Stakeholders**

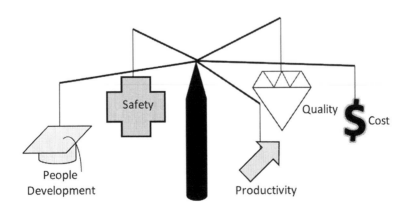

If any individual mission is removed or ignored, balance is lost everywhere. Each mission is dependent on the others for sustaining stability and thus achieving success.

Here are some real world examples of balance between the five missions. I recall vividly a time when I had a piece of painting automation down in one of my spray booths. This particular equipment was critical for ensuring the quality of the completed vehicle, but prior to my time as the general manager, it had been backed up manually several times. Before backing up the equipment manually on this particular occasion, I asked my engineering staff how we could guarantee that the manual operation would produce the same quality as the automated process. Their response was that this couldn't be done practically because to confirm the quality on every vehicle would require extensive downtime. We could visually "qualify" that the quality was OK, but there was no way to measure it and keep pace with our production rates. In my mind, this was a compromise that threw the five-mission scale out of balance. If we initiated the manual backup process, we would be risking quality for the sake of productivity. Maybe no customer would have ever detected this issue, but my responsibility to these stakeholders was to provide the best quality regardless of what else was going on in my paint shop. So my final direction was to either repair the automation or find a better, faster way to assess the quality of each manually processed vehicle. We ended up repairing the equipment without going into backup mode, and as a result, we experienced extensive downtime that day. The paint shop actually caused our customer in the final assembly process to run out of vehicles (a clear violation of TPS and JIT), but we made our ultimate decision based on a balanced support for all of our stakeholders.

Another example involved a situation where I had transferred several people out of my department to accommodate some movement for their career development. This left various holes in my organization, and I was left with two options. I could choose the quick and easy method of plugging the holes with someone who already had the skills and experience to perform the work, or I could take the longer path of using this as a development opportunity. In this particular case, I chose the employee development opportunity in spite of the fact that this option was less cost-effective. Let's face it, developing employees is an investment. There's just no two ways around this. Training takes time and money, people need time to become proficient with their new work, and the overall organization tends to lose a little momentum when people are learning new roles and developing new skills. So where's the balance? Employee development must be a priority just like reducing cost is a priority. As I said earlier, development is an investment versus the immediate cost benefits of stabilizing operations by utilizing people with existing skills and talents. So perhaps the balance is in taking a long-term versus a short-term cost perspective. In the end, the employee development opportunity will also yield improved commitment and job satisfaction for employees and increase the overall skill and knowledge base of the company.

My final point in this chapter is that knowing and committing to stakeholders is a long-term approach for success and viability. On the one hand, if you are a venture capitalist considering a Lean transformation so you can quickly improve the profit potential for an investment enterprise, then your stakeholders will be relatively limited. If this scenario describes your interest in TPS, then I would recommend using the "car detailing" approach toward implementation. Not sure what that is? Well, I'm confident that just about everyone has either bought or sold a used car in the past. And as such, you're probably familiar with the concept that what looks good usually sells first. Two identical cars sitting side by side will sell differently if one of them has been "detailed" or cleaned up to look nice. To make your business look "detailed," you can put up some TPS banners, do some quick 4S activity, and reduce a couple of dozen processes to improve labor costs. The fact that the company won't actually be any better won't matter because it will look better to your prospective buyers. Don't let taking this approach make you feel bad or cheap. We all do it when we sell a car.

If, on the other hand, you are a CEO or a senior manager of a small, privately owned company that plans to be in business for the next one hundred years, you're going to have dozens of stakeholders relying on your success. If this best describes your situation, then I would definitely recommend that you spend some time considering the points in this chapter. Kiichiro Toyoda had a vision for his company, but he also envisioned a better world. I think he developed his company based on his desire to create a better world. This is the soil where the TPS seed was planted and nurtured, and I believe wholeheartedly that this is the only environment where the benefits from TPS will have long-term growth.

CHAPTER 4
CREATING SHARED VISION AND DIRECTION

If you wanted to learn more about leadership you probably would have picked a book written by a different author. My expertise is not in the field of leadership, so I won't pretend to be an authority in this area. I do, however, believe that it's important to discuss leadership to some extent in this chapter because leaders create vision and set direction for their business, whereas managers organize and focus the resources used to conduct business. Both roles are necessary in successful companies, and in a few cases, a good leader and a good manager can be one in the same person. All too often, however, I have seen good managers who can take the resources given to them and create masterful results, but they couldn't create a vision and a forward-thinking strategy if their life depended on it. Taking this a step further, the structure or hierarchy of most companies is based on levels of management (notice the root word—*manage*?). So where does the leadership come in? Are we to assume that someone who is managing well and progressing through the company ranks automatically has developed good leadership skills as well? I am a firm believer that managers and leaders are not the same, and they very rarely overlap skills. Great leaders are sometimes also great managers, but great managers are not necessarily great leaders.

So who cares? Leader vs. manager—isn't this six of one and half a dozen of the other? I don't think so. Leadership is required to create the vision, the long-term mission, and values of the organization. The values define what the company is all about and the vision brings purpose to the work. The vision summarizes for all of the stakeholders what is collectively of value to the organization and why it is important. When a great leader creates a vision, customers, employees, communities—every stakeholder can clearly understand the purpose for their collective effort and relationship. The key word here is purpose. I believe that a great leader will bring purpose and meaning to the work that the organization delivers.

One other key point is that you will find leaders at all levels of the company. Have you ever heard the expression "floor general" in reference to a leader on a sports team? In short, the floor general is the leader on the court, on the field, or wherever the game is being played. The floor general is a peer leader, he's not the coach. This is exactly what I mean by having leaders at all levels within your company. There are people that have the respect of their peers and can make things happen all throughout your organization. Knowing who these people are and tapping into their capability as leaders is something that you're definitely going to want to do. Floor generals will bring the most valuable meaning to work because they are seen as being credible by their peers. Down in the trenches where the real work is happening, people need to see coworkers at their same level who are living the vision of the company. Sure, it's great when the entire senior management team is all on the same page too, but peer leadership is much more valuable and meaningful for your employees. My advice is that you find the floor generals in your organization and that you recognize them as being core assets for your company.

Now that you've given ample consideration to who your stakeholders are, the leadership within your organization must create a vision to bring purpose to the work being performed. When this vision is shared and committed to by all of the stakeholders, the organization will be united in a single purpose. This is when you'll really see the full potential of your team. When everyone sees a common purpose and shared vision, you will have tapped into the hearts and the minds of your employees. All too often we only tap into the physical resources of our employees—what I refer to as the "hands" element (see figure 4.1). The true strength of your organization is much more than the physical ability of your employees. The point at which your employee's physical ability, their commitment, and their creativity overlap is where they will perform at their peak. Creating a shared company vision is the most effective means for tapping into that space with your employees.

Figure 4.1 **Tapping into the Total Essence of a Human**

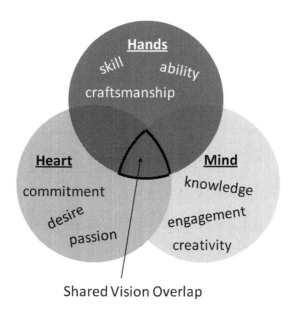

Shared Vision Overlap

But is simply creating the vision enough? A colleague of mine once told me that a vision without resources is nothing more than a daydream. Keep in mind that if you desire for your company's vision to come to fruition, you'll need to provide your people with the resources required to get the job done. One memorable vision is that of former President John F. Kennedy when on May 25, 1961, he announced to Congress the challenge of "landing a man on the moon." President Kennedy may have had the vision, but he had no idea how to make it become a reality. However, what he did have was the power to provide the necessary resources to the people who had the knowledge and skill to make a moon landing a reality. From the period of 1961 to 1975, the Apollo space program cost the United States more than $24 billion—a financial commitment larger than that of any other nation during peacetime. At the height of the program, there were more than 400,000 people and 20,000 industrial firms and universities working toward this goal. Clearly, President Kennedy understood that the achievement of this vision would not come without significant resource allocation, and although he never saw the first man walk on the moon, because his vision was shared by a nation, in 1969, the first man, an American named Neil Armstrong, walked on the moon's surface.

If vision provides the "what of work," then direction provides the "how of work." Setting direction for your company will convey the plan, the path, and the "how we're going to get where we're going" to the organization. Without the vision, the direction is meaningless. Who needs to know how they're going to get somewhere if they don't know where they're going? In a sense then, the vision is the destination, and the direction is the route you're going to take to get there. As with taking a trip across the country, the route can take many twists and turns, but the ending point should stay the same. One driver might prefer to stay on the interstates and another on two-lane highways, but the key point is that both routes eventually will arrive at the same destination. The differences in route selection, however, may determine what resources are required to reach the final destination. The leadership objective is to select the direction that best suits the resources at your company's disposal.

Have you ever been in an organization where there were lots of directions being parceled out, but the destination was either unknown or it seemed to be changing? This is much different than taking a detour. Direction without vision will exhaust your workforce and leave them doubting the company's leadership ability. On the other hand, consistent direction toward a shared vision will motivate a workforce and strengthen trust in leadership—even when slight deviations in direction are necessary due to unforeseen changes in the business environment.

When the economy went in the tank beginning in 2008, the automotive industry suffered tremendously—losing over 25% of their sales in a single year. Perhaps other lower margin, lower investment, or lower lead time industries may have been able to weather the severity of this economic downturn, but in the automotive world this was a very extreme condition. I can say with all honesty that it would have been very easy for Toyota to lose sight of their vision and maybe even shed a few stakeholders at this time, but they didn't. Toyota stayed true to their beliefs in the Toyota Way—continuous improvement and respect for people, but their approach or direction did have to change due to the severe business conditions they were now facing. One way Toyota showed respect for their employees was by providing them with job security and great pay and benefits. During the economic downturn, when many competitors were scaling back operations, Toyota kept all of their team members employed even when this meant shutting down operations and paying them to perform nonprofitable work. Yes, this expense and the loss of revenue forced Toyota to look at other ways to reduce cost such as forgoing pay advances and bonuses for a period of time, but overall, the Toyota Way value of respecting people stayed intact.

But that example is more about the values of Toyota versus the vision of Toyota—how was the vision affected by the downturn? Well, Toyota was also very well known at this time for their work with hybrid vehicles and alternate fuel sources. During the time between 2008 and 2010, the most severe portion of the economic downturn, Toyota continued to spend tens of millions of dollars pursuing research and development in both of these key areas. Toyota also continued to invest in tooling and facilities to increase hybrid battery production, allowing them to offer hybrid options for more of their vehicle lineup. The vision of Toyota to be a leader in the automotive industry in "green technology" never wavered. Sure, maybe some of the decisions were scrutinized more for cost, and in some cases, plans had to be delayed (i.e., a different route selected), but the final destination never changed.

Another element of Toyota's operations that is much different from typical, Western style business is the practice of "consensus management." Within Toyota, decisions are rarely made by a single person, and when they are, the decisions have been made only after that person has been counseled by many different stakeholders. The basic premise of this management philosophy is similar to the concept of "the wisdom of crowds"—no one person can possibly know everything, and therefore, getting more facts, opinions, and perspectives can only improve the quality of decision-making. Setting direction by gaining consensus is a key characteristic of Toyota's culture because it's one method used to provide inclusion for employees at all levels of the organization.

The process used by Toyota management to set short—to midterm direction is called *hoshin*. Loosely translated, a hoshin is a business plan, and typically they are created in either one year or five year versions. As you would expect from the names, the one-year hoshin sets direction for the current business year while the five-year hoshin looks ahead to the next five fiscal years. In both cases, the company vision would already have been set, and the management team would meet collectively to share ideas, opinions, and perspectives on how best to achieve this vision. Was this a democracy? Did people vote on which ideas they liked the best? Typically no, but this is a great opportunity to highlight another key element of Toyota's values and an area where differing opinion exists even within Toyota—how is consensus reached?

First and most importantly, I believe that Toyota employees would say that integral to the value of "respecting people" is the opportunity for everyone's opinions and perspectives to be freely heard and understood. In other words, Toyota wants all employees to feel as though they have a voice in their process and in their company. I personally believe that this is also what "consensus management" should be about—giving people an opportunity to voice their opinions and ideas while being respectful of the fact that we all have different perspectives. For me, consensus management means finding direction within a vastly diverse organization while seeking out the best and most effective ideas and solutions. To others within Toyota, however, consensus management means setting direction while including pieces of everyone's ideas in the final solution or outcome. This latter approach requires making compromises in order to create inclusion for everyone.

As you may have already concluded, these two approaches are vastly different and somewhat opposing. The approach that I favored, hearing everyone's ideas and then picking the best to move forward, was not considered the best form of consensus management because at the end of the day, not everyone had equal equity in the direction that was set. On the other hand, the approach of using bits and pieces of everyone's ideas, while inclusive, tended to miss the mark on effectiveness. So which approach was correct? Who knows? I can only answer for myself. As a leader, I felt like listening to everyone's ideas and giving them equal opportunity to provide input was a fair way to gain consensus. I would eventually have to disseminate the information and set the ultimate direction based on the counseling that I received, but I considered this to be respectful to the employees, fair, and consistent. I also felt like this was the timeliest approach to making decisions. Given the alternative approach of using bits and pieces of everyone's ideas, sometimes what seemed like a "no-brainer" decision could wind up taking months to make. Politically, this second approach served its constituents well because they were seen as people who could compromise, find common ground. Either way, to set direction, eventually, someone is going to have to step up and make a decision—consensus or not.

Now back to the hoshin. The one-year hoshin would only include immediate direction for new items moving the business one step closer to reaching the ultimate vision. The concept is that a more specific, detailed explanation would be required for initiatives being introduced for the first time. Any business practice that was considered normal, carryover, or "standard operating procedures" would not be spelled out in the hoshin. The one-year hoshin would also include metrics for setting clear targets and for measuring progress during the course of the fiscal year. The use of hoshin targets will be discussed in greater detail later in chapters 8–11, but for now, we'll summarize the purpose of target setting by stating that the targets create goal alignment within the organization.

The five-year hoshin was used to create some structure and a logical pattern for the forecasted future direction of the company. By building from the current direction of the one-year hoshin and working toward the ultimate vision of the company, a plan for the next five years could be constructed. Progressions of goals and targets would be extrapolated based on current conditions compared with the desired conditions five years down the road. This target-forecasting approach created an even deeper alignment throughout the organization by allowing employees at all levels to understand the longer-term expectations for performance. Nothing on the five-year hoshin was written in stone. All plans were subject to change based on potentially changing business conditions (both externally and inside the company), but the five-year hoshin did provide the best approximation for future direction based on the current business conditions and the best assumptions of future conditions.

Once the direction has been set and decisions have been made, how is information shared within your organization? Is a memo sent out? Is there a company policy or procedure handbook that is sent to your employees' homes? Do your supervisors depend on word of mouth to communicate direction and strategy? Perhaps a combination of multiple methods is used depending on the level or the significance of the direction or the decision. The most critical element of communicating to your team is that you provide some outlet for meaningful, two-way communication. One-way communication is great for letting your employees know what the menu is this week in the cafeteria, but if you want to understand and capture the hearts and minds of your employees, you'll need to create a culture of two-way communication.

There are, of course, other elements of communication that improve effectiveness, such as the timeliness, the tone, the relevance, the character, and the trust factor of the person delivering the communication, etc. In the Toyota culture, none of this is more important than giving the team members a voice in what is happening in their company (it is after all their company too—we identified team members as stakeholders). Two-way communication should ensure that anyone who wants to make comments regarding direction and decisions has that option. Perhaps this opportunity is facilitated by some open forum. Within Toyota, this was done frequently in both small group meetings with upper management and within "town hall" style meetings with bigger groups. Sometimes people would be hesitant to voice their opinions and provide feedback in a group setting, so other venues for communication may also be necessary. Consider how you can make time for one-on-one discussions between supervisors and their employees. As a last alternative, you might also want to consider providing an anonymous means for employees to provide feedback to management such as suggestion boxes or voice mailboxes. Although not strictly considered two-way communications, these methods can provide necessary insight into how your employees feel about the company's current direction.

In summary, without leadership there can be no vision and direction for your business. Also, the best managers are not necessarily the best leaders. To understand more about the differences between leadership and management I would suggest that you consider picking up a book by an expert in this field such as Stephen Covey, Ken Blanchard, or John C. Maxwell. For my own purposes it's critical for me to convey to you that vision and direction are integral to successfully deploying TPS in a Toyota Way culture. Sharing that vision and direction throughout your workforce will promote engagement that will allow TPS to grow and flourish. As you will hear me say many times in this text, TPS will not be sustainable without engagement of employees. I will discuss other techniques for engaging employees in future chapters of the book.

CHAPTER 5

KEEP STRATEGIES SIMPLE

Now that you have more insight regarding who your stakeholders are and you have developed a shared vision for your company, my advice for you is to not over-think how to deploy your business strategy. On the surface, it might appear that TPS and the Toyota Way are complex and detailed, but honestly, the beauty lies in their simplicity. When you understand "why" you are conducting your business, and you have a purpose in "what" your business would like to accomplish, the "how" should become fairly obvious—understand your core business and dedicate your resources to becoming the very best at what it is you are committed to doing.

The other day, I was on the phone with an employee of Amazon, and I asked him what got people excited about working there. He said that he got the most enjoyment from speaking with customers who were genuinely pleased with their service. He went on to explain that most customers have pretty basic expectations when dealing with Amazon—they want to shop efficiently, they expect to pay low prices, they want what they purchased quickly, and they expect what they purchased to be problem-free when it is delivered. What he said most customers don't understand is the complexity behind the logistics that allows all of this to happen. Perhaps you believe that this is some IT (information technology) magic, but in fact, Amazon's operational effectiveness is in their vast logistics and distribution systems. I took the fact that customers do not recognize the logistics complexity as a huge compliment to Amazon. They are so good at their core business that it becomes imperceptible to their customers. This is precisely what I mean by "keep it simple"—understand what your stakeholders expect and then focus on the few items that will bring operational effectiveness to your core business.

In the Amazon example, I'm not implying that logistics is simple. What I'm trying to say is that they understand who their stakeholders are, they have a vision regarding customer satisfaction, and they have focused on the operational effectiveness of logistics and distribution to pull it all together. At the end of the day, customers only remember the experience they had while ordering and receiving their products. Everything in between is invisible to Amazon's customers.

The reason I've included this chapter in my book is that I've seen how complicated a business can get—quickly and seemingly out of control. Although I'm jumping ahead a little, I must divulge the reason for needless complication and complexity entering into your operations—poor problem solving. We're going to discuss problem solving techniques and applications with TPS in chapter 8, but for the purposes of "keeping it simple," I need to introduce the concept of how poor problem solving creates complexity.

If you've worked at a company for ten to fifteen years, you may recall a time when a process came full circle. You know, when you were doing something back in the good old days, but for one reason or another someone decided that your process or system needed to change. Through many trials and errors (or attempted problem solving I should say) the process was modified again and again until one day someone finally said, "Hey, why don't we go back to doing it the old way?" Everyone will look around and try to remember why you stopped doing it that way to begin with. Now that you've tried a dozen other methods, it seems like the original process may have actually been the best. In the meantime, by changing the process and adding more steps, more checks, additional paperwork, more reports, etc., what you actually have accomplished is adding complexity but no real benefit. This is what happens when problem solving is not done well.

I'm speaking totally from my own experience here. I can recall times when business objectives were not being met at my plant, so the immediate thought was, "We need to try something else." In other words, the implication was that we're not doing enough versus we're not doing what we're supposed to be doing. Toyota was notorious for this type of thinking, and it drove me crazy. Yes, the company that prides itself in great problem solving also made knee-jerk decisions and didn't practice what they preached. About every other year at the time when business plans (hoshins) were being developed, someone would invariably bring up the idea of "getting back to the basics." It happened just like clockwork. The company's officers would nod their heads and begin to discuss in detail how great the basic, simple processes of the past worked. Meanwhile, I would do my best to bite my tongue (which rarely worked). In most cases, this was the same group that did no problem solving and mandated that more and more complexity be added to the processes and systems to begin with.

When you get to the point that you're questioning why you changed something in your operations, this may be a sign that you've missed some problem solving opportunities. I'm not saying that you never will or never should expect to make a mistake. We all make some wrong decisions. I do, however, assume that when making a poor decision that the error was made by selecting an ineffective problem solution, not that you were solving the wrong problem to begin with. The latter situation is where you'll get yourself in trouble—solving the wrong problem and/or solving a problem that's not really a problem at all.

My high school football coach said something once that has stuck with me for almost thirty years. One Saturday morning, we were watching the game film from the night before. We got our butts kicked pretty good by a cross-town rival, so the atmosphere was a little tense to say the least. As always, the coach would watch each play and then rewind and watch it again until he saw what every player on the field had done. This particular time, he asked one of the linemen why he blocked the way he had (or actually not blocked at all—it was a trick question). Presumably not knowing what to say, the guy simply said, "I don't know." The coach leaned back and thought for a moment and said, "Well, that's OK. I can fix 'I don't know,' but I can't fix 'I don't care.'" The more time I've spent working with people, the more I understand what my coach was saying—is the problem skill or will? When you're not getting the results that you want, it is entirely possible that organizationally you have a skill issue or that your process is no good. In this case, the problem that must be solved becomes obvious. On the other hand, if the problem is a "will" issue, you can train and modify the process all you want to and it's not going to improve the results. I believe this is the main reason for poor problem solving and adding needless complexity to your operations. Do your homework. Understand if the problem is "skill" or "will" before you start piling new systems into your business.

My final advice about simplicity is this—my observation has been that most people cannot perform simultaneous tasks well (and this includes both mental and physical tasks). I believe that people, even the most gifted and talented people, can only concern themselves with about three or four things at any given time. Let's not forget that our employees have personal lives, and it would be impossible for people to leave everything at the door when they walk into work. Whether someone is concerned about a situation with a family member, a financial problem, or possibly even something as simple as a busy weekend coming up, most employees have something on their mind besides what is happening at work. It's just human nature, and I believe that we need to accept this fact when we set expectations for our employees. How much can we or should we reasonably expect from someone? Maybe the correct answer is—it depends. It depends on the 4As and where any individual is within the 4A model (Don't get excited. An explanation of the 4As is coming up in the next chapter). But we also shouldn't weigh our employees down with needless complexity and bureaucracy that brings no true value to our core business.

"Keeping it simple" means giving our employees a better chance at being successful by not creating unwanted distractions and meaningless work. Look around your organization, or even better, ask your employees if they believe that some portion of their work is non-value added. I'm not talking about work that is unpopular or difficult, I'm talking about work that your employees could skip altogether and no one would even know the difference. Maybe the work is a report or a document that takes hours to produce but it's only briefly reviewed and by only a few members of management. Maybe the non-value work involves preparing for a meeting that has no real purpose or defined intention. When people are concentrating on this type of work, when do they have time to focus on the core business that really matters? No person's capacity is limitless. You must accept that if your employees are worrying about trivial things, they are not paying attention to what really matters.

So keep it simple. Understand your stakeholders' expectations, clearly define your vision and your goals, and then proceed with strategies that are simple and focused. Your employees will have more success executing basic plans and strategies, and your company will benefit from the employees' success.

CHAPTER 6

THE 4As OF SUCCESSFUL PERFORMANCE

The Toyota Production System is very much a management system. What do I mean by that? Most people reading this book have probably done their homework when it comes to managing an organization. Why else would you be reading another book about TPS if you weren't already a "lifelong learner" seeking out more tools for your management toolbox? This being the case, I'm also confident that you have studied and understand quite well the differences between "management" and "leadership" as I discussed in some detail in chapter 4. People much smarter than I am can help you to define these two words, but for the sake of this book, I will tell you that TPS has little to do with leadership. My experience with Toyota, in particular with the Japanese within Toyota, is that the term *leadership* is not often used. Yes, there are some managers at Toyota who are also good leaders, but in general they didn't become good leaders due to development within the Toyota organization. Either they learned these behaviors and techniques prior to coming to Toyota or they too were lifelong learners who gained expertise in leadership on their own while working at Toyota.

The principles of TPS are based on sound management. In other words, within TPS there are systems and processes that must be taught, understood, and put into practice. Once in place these systems and processes must then be checked and measured, and a cycle of continuous improvement initiated. What I've just described is a form of management, and within Toyota it is referred to as the plan–do–check–action or P–D–C–A cycle (illustrated in figure 6.1). In my opinion, there is no simpler or more elegant management process. Admittedly, however, the terms *plan*, *do*, *check*, and *action* are somewhat vague and certainly open to interpretation. So what does P–D–C–A management look like in practical terms and how is it used?

Figure 6.1   **The P–D–C–A Cycle of Management**

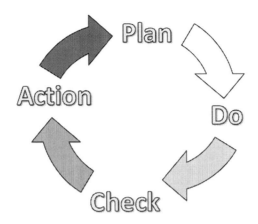

As I discussed in the "Background" section, Toyota passes information and knowledge through a process of OJD—or on-the-job development. This process generally consists of close interaction between a teacher and a learner (almost always between a superior and a subordinate) with hands-on, experiential teaching opportunities. As a new Toyota employee, one could expect to be taught this P–D–C–A cycle of management in such a manner. I was no exception to this rule. I spent many a production day on the manufacturing floor with Japanese trainers explaining the details of how to manage a production area using P–D–C–A. For example: Let's say that a defect appeared on a completed vehicle. First, we would verify the plan for producing that vehicle by referring to the standardized work that we discussed in the "TPS Basics" section. Each process on the manufacturing floor had a written set of instructions that every team member was trained to follow. To begin the P–D–C–A cycle, we would obtain the standardized work (generally kept near the production work site) and review it for completeness. We would confirm that the written instruction for the team member was thorough in detail, simple to understand, and visual in nature.

The do of standardized work consists of performing the process itself—the use of the standardized work by the team member. From the perspective of understanding why there was a defect produced by any given process, the check and the do would for all intents and purposes be combined. In other words, while the team member was performing the standardized work, I as the supervisor would check (observe) the process. I would use the written documents (the plan) to confirm (the check) the team member's performance (the do). In addition to observing the team member while performing his process, other parts of the check might include confirming the level of training the team member received for this process or possibly even checking the defect history for any given team member. Because team members rotate between processes during the course of a production shift, the rotation log might be checked to verify which team member was performing the process at the time the defect occurred. All of this confirmation activity would qualify as the check of the P–D–C–A for the defect that had been created.

The final step involves the action. This is where I found the most significant differences—the outcome from interactions between Japanese and the U.S. management and their respective employees. In Japan, the nonconformances found during the process check would be communicated to the team member, and in general, that would be the end of the discussion. Sure, there might be some slight modifications or additions made to the standardized work as a result of the investigation findings, but that's all it would take to correct the situation. In Japan, the team members (again, in general terms) understand the plan, and they follow it to the letter. Of course, this isn't a perfect assessment. After all, I visited Japanese plants frequently during my employment with Toyota, but I never managed in one personally. I merely observed the Japanese team members performing standardized work when I visited another Toyota site, and I routinely received instruction from Japanese trainers who did actually manage in these plants.

So what was different in the U.S.? Using the example above as a reference, the P–D–C part of this activity would pretty well be the same regardless of whether completed in a Japanese or a U.S. plant. The biggest difference was in the action or outcome from the process confirmation. In some cases, the method of informing, coaching, reinstructing, and clarifying expectations used by the Japanese would also work in the U.S. plant. However, this wasn't always the case. The Japanese approach works well when the employee has a "skill" issue, but if the real problem is a "will" issue, this approach may not work. Over and over again, I began to ask myself—are defects being created due to a skill or a will issue? In other words, is the problem that the team members don't know what to do, or is the problem that the team members don't care about what they are doing? (Remember my high school football coach's comments?)

The problem was that I had no way to differentiate between team members who lacked skill and who lacked will. However, I didn't want to assume that people weren't capable because they simply didn't care. I wanted to create a system for performance management that would ensure the success of the team members by starting at the very beginning of their skill development. I studied what I believed to be the keys areas for performance success, created a clever acronym, and the 4As became the method I used to instruct my organization in effective performance management.

The 4As stand for ability, authority, alignment, and accountability. I believed that without some clear method to manage the performance behaviors observed while conducting a P–D–C–A cycle, the final outcome or the action would rarely ever address the actual problem—the root cause if you will. How did we know this? We knew this because we were having the same types of problems over and over again within a work environment where standard processes, training, and a culture for TPS and continuous improvement were supposed to be present. In Japan, the management process is pretty simple and straightforward—tell the team members what they need to do, show them how to do it, and then expect that they will do this each and every time from that point forward.

My practical observation, however, is that this method for managing the Toyota Production System in a Western culture (or at least in the U.S.) just doesn't work. Is it because U.S. employees can't perform standard processes? No, not at all. Is it because U.S. employees don't care about their job? No, this isn't the case either. So what's the big difference? Why does TPS work so well in Japan (and in countries such as Mexico, Taiwan, and Thailand I might add), but in the U.S., the system of TPS is more difficult to implement? The answer that I've found is that in the U.S. employees want to find meaning in their work. Application of TPS requires a significant amount of effort in the form of discipline to execute detailed processes. If workers cannot find some connection between the effort and the outcome, they generally won't put forth the effort—at least not for long. If, on the other hand, the effort can be tied back to some purpose, tangible benefit, or positive outcome for the team members, they will perform even the most detailed standardized work and engage in their process.

To understand more about how I came to this conclusion, I need to give a brief history lesson of Toyota's first experiences with a North American workforce. When Toyota began their first solely managed operations in the U.S., they drew from the experience gained from managing both in Japan and at their joint venture with General Motors—NUMMI (New United Motor Manufacturing Inc.). Toyota, being no different than any other transplant automotive business starting in the U.S., did not want the influence of a union in their operation. Although the joint venture at NUMMI did have a union workforce, the environment was created out of concessions from the UAW in order to bring manufacturing jobs back to a GM/UAW plant that had been closed in Fremont, California. In these concessions, the union agreed to more flexible working conditions, team concepts, and fewer job classifications—all of which were necessary for Toyota to successfully implement TPS. The concession from Toyota was that they would enter this partnership with both GM and the UAW by hiring back employees who were previously laid off from the closed GM plant.

When Toyota decided to strike out alone with a solely owned and managed plant within the U.S., the idea of starting with UAW support never crossed their minds. They wanted to ensure the maximum flexibility of their workforce, so they located the plant in a historically union-free area—Georgetown, Kentucky. To keep the team members neutral to unions, Toyota used pay scales and benefits similar to those of the UAW competitor plants. In addition, TMM (Toyota Motor Manufacturing or Toyota Motor Manufacturing, Kentucky—TMMK as it is known today) also created many attractive, monetary reward systems for their team members. These included paid suggestion systems, car giveaways for perfect attendance, prize giveaways for special events in the plant, cafeteria cash for random "good acts" of performance, and the list goes on and on.

Now allow me to explain why this background information is so important in the context of performance management. I believe that when Toyota began operations at TMMK, they artificially created a high performance culture through generous giving and, in essence, "purchased" the commitment of their team members. The first people who worked at TMMK were making more money than anyone else in manufacturing in the surrounding area. The culture felt good to them because they were financially rewarded for many of the things that they did, and they did these things very well I might add. Nonetheless, my takeaway from this is simple—Toyota didn't want a union, and to avoid having one, they were willing to give "extras" to team members to ensure their flexibility to perform using TPS philosophies.

TMMK was the first of six solely owned vehicle assembly plants located within North America, and none of the other plants followed the pay and incentive model used by TMMK. This was due in part because by the mid—to late 1990s when the other plants were being built, Toyota realized that the UAW was less of a threat to organize transplants. After all, none of the other transplants (Nissan, Honda, Isuzu, etc.) had UAW representation, and the UAW within the Big Three auto manufacturers (GM, Ford, and Chrysler) was shrinking every year due to plant closings and downsizing. Mostly, however, I believe that Toyota learned some very valuable lessons from their initial plant startup at TMMK. Specifically, Toyota learned that team members, when treated using Toyota Way values, would not want UAW representation. The respectful work environment at Toyota was bad soil for union-organizing efforts. Also, the pay and incentives that were part of TMMK's compensation package for team members were really not required to "persuade" team members to follow TPS strategies. Pay at these other Toyota facilities was still very good (the best job in town so to speak) and most employees felt blessed and grateful for the pay and benefits they received. So the remainder of the North American Toyota facilities did not go overboard with labor incentives because they were tactically not necessary.

Time to bring it home—so what's the bottom line? Over a period of twenty-five years, Toyota has seen the light, and the realization is that they could not keep up with the wages and "perks" that the TMMK team members enjoyed any longer. The recession during the 2008–2010 time period had a significant impact on all of the automobile makers, and Toyota was no exception. Specifically, the TMMK plant was particularly hard hit because their team members had the most to lose financially. What I observed during this time was that as financial perks were reduced or eliminated from the TMMK employees, the commitment of the team members to perform according to the Toyota Production System also declined. Was this some form of rebellion against Toyota? Some team members would say that it was, but others would deny this emphatically. What I can tell you from personal experience is that the effort level went down, and TPS became much more difficult to follow because team members were disengaged from the company.

So if your company has bottomless pockets and you can afford to buy your worker's commitment, then you're in pretty good shape for implementing TPS. In fact, if you have this kind of money, you may not even need TPS. If, on the other hand, you want to implement TPS to reduce your cost, it will be imperative that you find some way to engage your employees using methods other than purely financial incentives. One thing for certain is that you will not be effective in sustaining your TPS efforts without engaged employees—this is a fact. Using this 4As method is one possible solution to creating a culture between your team and your management where everyone feels empowered and engaged. During the remainder of this chapter I will discuss the elements of my 4A approach along with how it can be practically applied to support TPS initiatives in your company.

First, please understand that the 4As should be considered as one process with four unique steps. Each step stands alone, and there is a definite progression of steps building upon each other. It is for this reason that the 4As have been listed in the order of ability, authority, alignment, and accountability—this is the sequence in which the steps must be implemented. There are some exceptions and some situations where multiple steps will be taken simultaneously, but the basic premise of this process is that the steps should be completed in this order. The 4A process and the subsequent order of these four steps was developed by closely observing Toyota team members who performed well and exhibited high levels of engagement (i.e., commitment to the company, willingness to improve their processes, and flexibility to place the team's needs above their own). Conversely, I also learned from those who struggled to perform and lacked commitment and job satisfaction. By assessing both of these conditions, I concluded that everyone has basic needs for development in order to achieve peak performance. Additionally, maintaining the sequence of the 4A steps ensures that employees won't lose trust in management, become frustrated, and ultimately not reach their true potential.

The word *trust* here is very important. This is why the 4As should be approached like a process—a process which is well understood by both the person doing the development (we'll call this person the teacher from this point forward) and by the person being developed (referred to as the student from this point forward). By approaching these steps as a process, common, standard language and expectations can be set between the teacher and the student. My deep conviction is that inherently people want to perform well, and when they are not, something has gone seriously wrong in their personal development. By following the 4A process, I have found that those who genuinely lack "skill" can be developed both effectively and efficiently, and those employees who lack "will" cannot hide behind the "I don't know" excuses any longer.

1) *Ability*—Just as you might suspect, ability describes the core knowledge and skill that will be required to perform your job. The level of required ability at this point is not relevant. What is relevant is that the student must acquire some level of skill and knowledge prior to beginning any real work. Sounds simple, but I can tell you from both personal experience and from observation that many people are thrown into a work setting without even the most rudimentary education or instruction. It's the old "sink-or-swim" technique of learning, and frankly, it doesn't work. Well, I guess it does work if your goal is to completely frustrate your employees and make them feel incompetent. On the other hand, if you're trying to improve your company's performance by employing the most successful individuals you possibly can, the "sink-or-swim" method is not going to be the best choice for developing your people.

The desired level of ability for each employee will vary depending on the work that must be performed. Because standardized work is generally broken into small work segments or elements, it would be logical and perhaps even desirable that the teaching/learning cycle be broken into small pieces as well. The work can then be learned and practiced one step at a time and built upon progressively as each step is mastered. When training is performed using standardized work, it is important to ensure that the documents contain sufficient written and visual detail to instruct the student.

Finally, don't think that providing employees with only the "bare essential" instruction is a formula for success. Complete knowledge is rooted in complete understanding. Minimal instruction will yield minimal learning and, thus, poor to average performance. Is your company's rally cry for success "Let's be average!"? If so, the minimum instruction method will quickly give you the performance results that you're looking for. If, on the other hand, your goal is to achieve world-class performance results, then I would suggest that you provide your workers with world-class capability.

Standardized work can provide great instructions for training, but what about knack items? You know, those little finesse skills that are learned over time once you've performed a job repetitively? Are these skills identified and taught in standardized work? What about "if not followed" key points—are they included in the standardized work? Sometimes to grasp the correct method or technique, it's best to teach what the consequences are if the proper steps are not followed. For example: "Failure to tighten this bolt properly could result in a brake system failure and possible injury or fatality of the customer." This is a pretty enlightening "if not followed" key point, wouldn't you say?

I can remember an instance when one of my team leaders was teaching standardized work for a sealer application and finishing process in our paint shop. The teacher provided instruction for the student on the proper location, application, and finishing of the sealer per the standardized work for the job. There was also a note in the standardized work next to one of the instructions stating that this process was a "delta" process. When the student asked the teacher what this meant, he replied that the process was important and needed to be followed exactly as it was written. Well, that was partially true, but what the "delta" coding for the process actually referred to was a critical torque requirement for a fastener in this location. You see, if even a small amount of sealer was applied where the strut installed onto the body, there was a potential for the fastener connecting the strut to become loose over time (i.e., the sealer would create a "soft" or under-torque condition when the bolt was tightened later in the assembly process). When both the teacher and the student were told the detailed meaning of this "delta" identification, they immediately and completely understood why this work instruction was so important.

2) *Authority*—Because the 4As are basically an acronym for a performance and development model, I needed four words all beginning with the letter "A" that roughly described the four steps of the process. The term *authority* for step 2 offers the most general description of the 4As, but I think I can bring it home for you with this explanation. Initially, my thinking was along the lines of giving people the freedom to perform the work that they have now been trained to do (remembering that the ability step came first). After all, there's nothing worse than being taught how to perform your work only to have someone stand over top of you and micromanage. My approach has always been similar to what I've observed in successful sports teams—let's say a football team. Each position has its own unique responsibility; the linemen block, the running backs run the ball and block for the quarterback, the quarterback leads the offense, etc. Once all the players have the ability to perform in their position, the rest of the team and the coaches need to step back and allow each person to do his respective job. A quarterback who is worried all the time about what the linemen are doing can't be a very successful quarterback. Even the coach has way too many responsibilities during a game to oversee what each individual player is doing. There's a time for reflection and film watching after the game, but during the game, each player must be allowed to use the ability that he has acquired.

Giving authority to a worker gives that person some confidence that you believe he can be successful. As the teacher and/or supervisor you can use discretion as to how much authority you hand over to any given employee. This is what I refer to as "defining the role" and this too is a key element of authority. The role definition creates the boundaries for authority. When explaining to a student that "this is what you can and cannot do," you are creating some space for him to own part of his work. Again, you decide the role. The key point is that you clearly identify the role and to that extent what authority you are giving the student/employee.

Giving and receiving authority can come with a price—it almost always does. With authority comes the space to make mistakes. That's right, once you give one of your students/employees the authority to operate within a defined role, you need to back off and let that person perform. To expect even the most skilled and capable people to not make mistakes is just not reasonable.

The truth is that all of us learn tremendously from our mistakes (especially when we're committed and motivated to do good work), and the TPS world is no different. Where do you think the concept of continuous improvement comes from? Can you improve something that is perfect? How do you kaizen a flawless process? Obviously, we don't want to encourage mistakes, and certain contingencies and risk management should be taken to ensure that mistakes do not have major consequences. Outside of this, we should manage mistakes like they are simply opportunities to improve. After all, that's exactly what they are when we approach them with a positive attitude and a willing heart and mind. The bottom line is that once you give authority to an employee who has the requisite amount of ability, get ready to live with the consequences.

Within a corporate culture where TPS principles are firmly rooted, authority must also include giving employees room to improve their process. All too often when problems arise in the workplace, the tendency is to turn to the "experts" to figure out what needs to be done. Who are the experts? Well, the management team for certain, and let's not forget about that "Lean team" of experts that you've put together—you know, the folks that had those two weeks of TPS and Six Sigma training? You may even bring in some technical or functional resources such as engineers to solve your most pressing issues. Trust me, there is a time and a place for all of these, but don't forget that your true "experts" are the employees that are performing the processes all day long.

Just put yourself in their shoes for a minute. What if you were struggling with some aspect of your work and your supervisor suggested that he help you out by bringing in a team of "experts" to solve your problem? How would that make you feel from a competency standpoint? What would your engagement and process ownership look like? People have the same needs to achieve job satisfaction and fulfillment in the workplace. We all need to feel like we have a voice in what we are being asked to do. When process improvements are required, start by getting input from the people closest to the process. This is the essence of giving employees authority in their work. Truly owning a process means owning everything—the current successes and failures as well as the future opportunities. From my experience, employees cannot feel authority without giving them the primary voice of their process.

The last point regarding authority was really already covered in the "TPS Basics" section, but it warrants repeating. One of the key elements of jidoka within TPS is the andon. Remember that the andon is a system which gives control of the process's progress to the worker. This is authority if I've ever seen it! Giving workers the power to stop a process when they detect a problem is the ultimate authority. Talk about empowerment! This is why the andon is such a critical element for jidoka. Empowering employees to be the eyes and ears in the process is the utmost level of authority. In doing so, you will have increased the employees' stake not only in their process, but also in the company. They are not just employees, they are process owners. If you want to throw a monkey wrench in your operations, take the andon away. Don't give your workers the authority to stop their processes or question what is good or bad with their work. Do this and you will kill the spirit of the process owner, and you'll be losing one of the single biggest advantages to operating your business with TPS principles. On the other hand, when you give your workers authority such as using the andon and create process ownership, you will begin to see the benefits of an organization that believes in continuous improvement, and you will have taken the first step toward building a fully engaged workforce.

3) *Alignment*—This may be the one step of my performance and development process that is superfluous within Toyota—at least within the Japanese plants. I say this because to me the Japanese culture in general seems so compliant to rules, systems, and processes that questioning, "Why is this important?" doesn't seem to be a concern to most Japanese workers. Here's an example to help rationalize my theory: I was once walking through one of the Toyota assembly plants in Japan and I saw a piece of very dangerous equipment with no guarding around it. Of course from a North American manager's viewpoint, this just didn't pass the sniff test. My first thought was that OSHA would have a field day with this kind of safety issue.

Later, I asked one of the Japanese trainers why this machine wasn't guarded, and he was genuinely confused by my question. So in true Toyota Way fashion, the trainer and I returned to the equipment *(genchi genbutsu)* and I showed him my machine guarding concern. Immediately, he pointed out that there was in fact a yellow caution line clearly painted around the perimeter of the machine. I told him that was great, but what if someone stuck a part of his body into the machine while it was cycling? What safeguard was there to protect a worker from the hazard of being crushed by the equipment when it cycled? Again, the trainer pointed to the yellow line and said that the yellow line means "don't cross—this is a dangerous place." You see, in the culture of the Japanese plants, yellow lines translate to "Danger, stay out!" and everyone was taught this. Once they were taught, everyone followed the rule, and no one would have ever crossed a yellow line for fear that he might be injured.

Wow! I immediately thought of about ten guys I knew who would be dead by now if that's how we ran our plants in the U.S. Heck, telling someone to not cross the yellow line was almost a sure way to entice the exact opposite behavior. Why such a difference? All I can say is that my experience with the Japanese culture is that they generally follow rules—to the letter! Here's my favorite example. The second time I traveled to Japan I was leading a group of new Toyota team members to be trained at our mother plant in Tahara. We arrived in the evening, and after a long, exhausting flight, a group of us decided that we wanted to unwind over a beer. So after meeting in the hotel lobby, we ventured out into the streets of Toyohashi looking for a *yakitori* or a snack bar. When we approached the first street intersection, there was already an elderly lady standing at the crosswalk. The crossing sign was red, but there wasn't a car for what seemed like miles. Again, it was late at night, and we were pretty much the only ones out and about with the exception of a few people who appeared to be coming home from some late shopping. Anxious to get our beer, and realizing that there was no imminent threat of being run over by a car, our entire group crossed the street against the direction of the red sign. Holy cow! You would have thought that we committed a felony. The few people who were out this late (including the elderly lady who we had just passed) gave us the stare down like you wouldn't believe. It was one of those "you-ugly-American" type stare downs that made you feel just terrible. From that point forward, we followed the pedestrian rules just like everyone else—and I mean everyone!

So people tend to follow rules and do what they're told in Japan. Believe this or choose not to, it's really not that important. I am merely trying to explain why at Toyota the concept of alignment was somewhat misunderstood or underemphasized by the Japanese staff. From their perspective—we have rules, and they should be followed. It's simple right? Maybe, but my experience has been that when people know why they are doing what they are doing, a bond of purpose is created bringing more meaning and ownership to workers. So alignment is just that—bringing purpose to work by explaining why the work has a greater meaning. What is a greater meaning? Well, maybe only you can answer this for your company, but for Toyota that greater meaning was always linked back to our hoshin or our business plan. As discussed in chapter 4, the hoshin was created and passed down by management for the purpose of outlining goals and strategies for the upcoming year. The hoshin was then used to break down goals and company targets to each section, department, group and, ultimately, every employee. This is one method that Toyota used to bring some alignment to every level of the organization.

Another way to create alignment is through use of the "team concept." Simply put, Toyota, like many other companies today, bundles employees into "teams" to create small work groups having common goals and values. When employees truly share these goals and values, you have created alignment—a team sharing a similar purpose, all working in the same direction. This is a powerful tool for building commitment and enthusiasm within your organization and at virtually no cost to the company. This team alignment also brings purpose to each worker's job because he now connects with the fact that his work impacts others. In other words, my job is important because you are depending on me. Remember the analogy about the football team? The same concept applies here. Each employee has unique work to perform, and everyone on the team is depending on each other to perform that work well—well enough to achieve a common goal.

Lastly, alignment is really the final element to creating employee commitment within your company. The "why of work" has long been recognized as a key attribute for employee engagement, improved job satisfaction, and an overall high level of commitment from employees. Some companies, however, feel that strong management is a viable option to having committed employees. If we looked at my Japanese culture image in the strictest sense, one might conclude that success can be achieved by having employees who follow good rules, systems and processes. This premise may in fact be true—at least for a short period of time. Success achieved by adherence to strict rules, policies, and systems requires a great deal of management discipline and perseverance. I developed the following model to visualize and communicate my concept regarding goal achievement based on the relationships between management capability and employee engagement (refer to figure 6.2).

Figure 6.2   **Understanding Why You Are Succeeding**

Management Capability	Employee Engagement	
	Committed	Compliant
Highly Skilled	Ideal Condition – Achievement of best results with continuous improvement.	Good Condition – Achievement of satisfactory results with some sustainment
Needs Development	Good Condition – Achievement of satisfactory results with some sustainment	No Good Condition – Cannot achieve desired performance for even a short time.

Based on my theory shown here, good to excellent performance results can be achieved in three of the four quadrants of this matrix. The final quadrant—"Needs Development" management coupled with "Compliant" employees will normally not return a favorable performance result. This is generally true because compliant employees are not fully engaged. They do not own their process and they will only give what is requested of them. Remember, these employees are functioning in a culture of rules, policies, and systems. They have not been conditioned to think for themselves. This isn't a destructive or subversive workforce. To the contrary—they have been trained to do exactly what you ask them to do and nothing more. When your management team is weakened due to attrition, rotations, or other organizational movement, your performance will suffer due to the loss of management capability.

The other obvious argument for having committed employees is that in a true TPS culture you are going to want employees that think for themselves, question the status quo, and look beyond their current set of circumstances. A workforce that merely "does what they're told" isn't going to get you where you're trying to go with TPS (continuous improvement that is). So by aligning your workforce with the "whys of work," you will build commitment to achieve shared goals. Isn't this what every successful company is trying to achieve?

4) *Accountability*—What a nasty word. Who really likes the word *accountability*? Later in my explanation of this fourth and final step of my performance and development model, I will introduce a more likeable word. For now we're going to

stick with accountability because I think it conjures up the initial associations that I want you as the reader to have—pressure, responsibility, and consequences.

Accountability simply means answerability and responsibility. That's basically it. My belief is that once you have all the skill and knowledge required to perform your work (ability), you have been given a definition of how you are to perform your work and the resources with which to do it (authority), and you understand why your work is important (alignment), it's time for you to step up and take responsibility for the outcome of your own work performance. Accountability is the catalyst for change for compliant workers. What? Perhaps you thought the 4As was going to help you create committed workers? After all, that is what I've been preaching for the past ten pages, but the likelihood that you're going to create an entire workforce of committed workers is slim to none. If you can get 80–85% of your workers committed through this process, you'll be doing great. The problem is that you can't successfully manage using TPS when only 80–85% of your workforce has "bought in." To achieve all of the goals (the roof of the TPS house) you'll need everyone on your team pulling in the same direction. Half or three-quarter performance isn't going to cut it with TPS, at least not over the long haul.

Tremendous effort and discipline are required in order for TPS principles to be applied effectively. If 75% of your employees are "all in" and the remainder are just kind of going through the motions (you know, putting in their eight hours and then hitting the parking lot like a flash of lightning), sooner or later that 25% is going to start adversely affecting your committed workforce. Maybe your team is strong enough to weather this type of scenario, but my experience has been that over time, if only part of the team is "all in" and committed, then eventually there are going to be some disgruntled employees. After all, is everyone going to benefit from the accomplishments of the exceptional 75% of your committed workforce? If so, eventually the 75% are going to start wondering why they work harder than the 25% (the compliant group) for the same benefits. If, however, the image of this scenario already has you thinking, "Well, I wouldn't compensate the workers the same. I would give the committed workers a bigger share of the benefits," then you're already thinking along the lines of accountability.

Another element of TPS that is important to remember and has significant relevance to the topic of accountability is kaizen. Toyota has always strongly believed that their team members are more than just "hourly workers." Sure, the assembly workers at Toyota are paid as nonexempt employees with hourly wages, but that's not what this statement means. What this means is that Toyota has higher expectations of their nonexempt employees than what might traditionally be considered of a "production worker." My own definition of the roles and responsibilities for a Toyota team member (an hourly employee that is) are as follows:

1) Always, regardless of the situation, all Toyota employees are to treat each other with dignity and respect.
2) When a team member's process is in motion, he is expected to follow standardized work.
3) All team members are expected to continuously improve (kaizen) their processes.

So back to the accountability connection—what's the incentive for a noncommitted team member to kaizen his or her process if there is no accountability? After all, if performance doesn't matter, why worry about improving? Talk about a trap for falling into the status quo—this is it! Again, you may be able to compensate for this for a short period of time *if* you have a strong and disciplined management team, but in the long run, you cannot manage kaizen in this way. In this situation, the management team will decide that it's easier for them to do the kaizen themselves rather than force someone who doesn't want to participate. This isn't true kaizen, the team members won't sustain the improvements, and the same problems will continue to come back over and over again. When the team member has no accountability, there are no consequences, and therefore, there is no reason for him to want to change and improve.

Keep in mind we're not talking about your committed employees here. Your committed employees are already "all in" and for them accountability looks more like acknowledgement. Ah, here's that other A-word I was telling you about. The positive form of accountability for your committed employees is acknowledgement. There is nothing more positive than genuine, honest, timely praise for work that is being performed well. Acknowledgement doesn't have to be in the form of monetary recognition—as a matter of fact, I would suggest that this type of acknowledgement be saved for only very special and unique performance accomplishments. Instead, you might consider some simple visual recognition for your highest performers such as a patch or a pin on their uniform or hat identifying them as a high performer. "Walls of Fame" with pictures of employees also work well for recognizing achievements. Even a simple handshake and some appreciation from you personally will go a long way to making the accountability/acknowledgement connection.

Trust me, this stuff works. Anyone who thinks that this method is nonsense might want to open his mind to a new approach. One of my favorite sayings is, "You can't learn anything if you already know everything." I can tell you from personal experience that using this method within Toyota helped me manage performance for both my committed and my compliant team members. Even when the culture conditions are optimal for deploying TPS as they are at Toyota, you will still need to apply techniques such as the 4As to achieve and sustain good performance and results.

Here's how I tested this system for the first time. I'm philosophically a Mr. Miyagi (from the *Karate Kid*) "wax on, wax off" kind of guy. Translation—I believe we can learn more complex ideas from simple applications. Toyota's North American plants are all "zero landfill" sites meaning that every effort is made to reuse or recycle waste. There are hundreds of waste streams within an automotive assembly plant, and before they can be recycled, the waste must be segregated. One of my responsibilities at TMMK was as the site's environmental director. On at least a monthly basis, I would review the plant's environmental KPIs (key performance indicators) with my staff. One of the KPIs used to measure our zero-landfill efforts was "waste segregation performance." This was an actual measurement of how well team members would separate different wastes into segregation containers. The data for the KPI was collected by one of the environmental staff who would audit every container's waste monthly for compliance.

Each time I reviewed our environmental performance, the result for the waste segregation KPI was significantly below target, and I just couldn't understand why separating trash was so difficult. We've all segregated recyclable waste to some extent—right? You know, put the paper in the paper bin, the plastic in the plastic bin, the glass in the glass bin, etc.? My strong conviction was this—if we can't do something simple like segregate our recyclable materials into the appropriate containers, what makes us think that we can build a car the right way? After all, isn't building a car much more difficult than throwing an aluminum can into the correct waste bin? I just couldn't get my arms around this lack of performance with such a seemingly simple process!

So in my areas of responsibility we began the 4A process for waste segregation. You may be asking yourself (as many of my colleagues did at the time), "Was waste segregation really your biggest problem and worthy of this type of effort?" My answer would be yes! Remember, I'm a Mr. Miyagi kind of thinker. The way I looked at it, our problem wasn't that we weren't segregating waste correctly. Our problem was that we didn't have the discipline (or the character and integrity) to do what needed to be done when we weren't being closely watched and managed. I extrapolated this to all aspects of our business, not just waste segregation. I used this situation as a platform to focus on some serious culture issues that I felt needed to be addressed.

Per the 4A model, we started with ability. We confirmed that every team member had information regarding what was recyclable and what was not recyclable. We confirmed that every area had the correct number of waste bins and that each bin was suitably designed for its intended purpose. We verified that the visual management and labeling was correct for each recycling location. In short, we covered every conceivable aspect of the ability step. All the while, our overall performance for waste segregation only improved slightly. However, I didn't get excited and start taking people to task. After all, we had only completed the first 4A step.

Next, we tackled the authority phase. We carefully instructed team members regarding our expectations for their role in waste segregation. In many cases, the recycling elements of processes were added to standardized work to emphasize the necessity of performing these work steps properly. We also made it clear to team members that we wanted them to "pull the andon" if they noticed issues with their recycling system—containers misplaced, full, etc. If there was any reason that a team member could not perform the necessary waste segregation work, we wanted to make certain that concerns were being bubbled up to management and being addressed quickly. Again, not much progress was made up to this point with the KPI performance. We stayed the course, however, and went on to step 3.

In the alignment step, we shared with team members why recycling was important by explaining the significance of the "zero-landfill" initiative for our company's corporate image. In order for the plant to achieve this target, each team member would need to do his part in waste segregation. We also touched on the broader environmental impact of landfills and pollution to emphasize the social need for change. Finally, we emphasized the cost of not recycling to our team members. Many of our recyclable wastes actually generated a revenue stream for the company. Additionally, several of the recyclable materials could be returned to suppliers and reused which helped to avoid costs. These tangible benefits were visualized by displaying them in the areas where the waste was being segregated as a reminder to team members. Unfortunately, there was still no appreciable performance improvement. The people who had been recycling were still recycling and only a few of the others were converted up to this point.

The final step was accountability. From the onset of this initiative I had invested dozens of hours and other resources to ensure that our team members could perform waste segregation successfully. The committed team members were doing just that, but we still hadn't achieved our goal (as measured and tracked by our environmental KPIs). Now, instead of confirming the segregation results on a monthly basis, I asked supervisors to start checking their waste daily—in some cases even more frequently. Initially, the supervisors were finding problems and correcting them by themselves. It was easier for them to simply move the materials from one container to the next than to confront a team member about why the material was in the wrong container to begin with. (Remember what I was saying earlier about compensating for the performance of compliant employees through strong management?) After a few weeks, our KPI results did improve, but my supervisors were getting very frustrated. I was being asked: "Why am I spending time digging through trash cans when we have much bigger issues to tackle?" and "I'm just a glorified trash man now, not a supervisor."

I respected their dilemma, but I didn't support their methods. In a monthly communication meeting, I told the supervisors that I wanted them to start having their team members sort through the recycling to ensure the segregation was done correctly—after work if necessary (and of course, they were to be paid for their time). After several of them tried this, the team members freaked out! They couldn't believe that we were making them stay after work to sort through the trash. This was after all "their time," and they felt we were not justified in keeping them late. My response—"You are being paid to segregate waste so the company can achieve our zero-waste initiative. You now have all the resources you need to do this work correctly the first time (i.e., when you throw the waste away). If you cannot segregate the recycling correctly the first time, you will need to do it again until it's done correctly." Once more, my "shared goal," the goal that we communicated to the team members when we took them through the 4A process, was to achieve our waste segregation target so our plant could achieve a zero-landfill status. This goal hadn't changed, but my approach to achieving it had.

Once, the team members were asked to stay after work and sort through the waste (a decision I might add that had our human resource department mighty upset), they began to point out problems that up to this time had not been mentioned. Examples included the following:

1) The lids of the bins are difficult to open when you have trash in your hands and/or the lids are getting messy because they are being handled while trash is in our hands (kaizen—foot-pedal-operated cans were installed).
2) We're not sure if this particular waste is recyclable (kaizen—better visuals and explanations were added to recycling locations).
3) Other people are walking by the common recycling areas, and they are the ones misusing the system (kaizen—groups were given exclusive control over their recycling areas by removing them from common locations within the plant).

None of the problems that the team members identified couldn't be resolved—at least once they had been exposed so we could work together and find the best solution. So what was the ultimate accountability for the team members? Was anyone fired? Of course not. The accountability was in the team members having to correct their own mistakes and during a time that they considered "their own" The results? My areas were the first to achieve the recycling segregation compliance target, and we maintained that favorable result each month after the 4A process had been completed. Overall, the company had not yet met their plantwide goal, but we were doing our part. Soon, other departments began to benchmark our methods.

One side note from my first application of the 4As has to do with the human relations side of the business. Earlier, I mentioned that the HR group was a little nervous about us asking team members to stay after work to sort through waste (and that's actually quite an understatement). Their concern was that we were violating one of the core Toyota Way principles—respect for people. Although I understood completely why they were upset, I did not agree with their interpretation of what respect for people meant in this situation. I believe wholeheartedly that the Toyota Way meaning of respect for people cannot exist without some level of accountability. Ideally, employees would have a high level of personal accountability, but we all realize that people have different values and priorities when it comes to work ethics. My opposition to HR's approach to the respect-for-people issue is that their focus was on the employees who were *not* performing versus those who were performing. It's true that everyone was required to stay after work regardless of whether or not they were segregating waste properly. Those who were following the rules understood why this was important. They shared the vision, and they actually put pressure on the noncommitted team members to get on board. Asking people to do work that they are capable of doing is not disrespectful when the 4A process is followed.

The 4A approach was born out of my personal belief that all people inherently want to perform well combined with the philosophies of the Toyota Way. Very few of us are satisfied with failure or with achieving mediocre results. We as management must ensure that our employees have all of the resources necessary to be successful. When neglecting to do this, we not only set our committed employees up for failure, but we also enable any noncommitted employees by giving them an excuse for not performing. Give people what they need to be successful, set expectations and goals, bring meaning to their work, and then hold them accountable for utilizing the resources you have given them. When applied fairly and consistently, using the 4A approach will allow both employee and company success.

CHAPTER 7

THE IMPORTANCE
OF VALUING EMPLOYEES

As I've already mentioned several times, respect for people is one of the core values of the Toyota Way. This belief has also become part of my own personal core value system over the years, and I'd like to take some time in this chapter to explain why valuing your employees should matter to you—especially if you want to transform your business using Lean or TPS principles. In today's business world, one would hope that this thinking is becoming mainstream, but the more I speak with people who work outside of Toyota, the more I have come to realize that there are still many opportunities to improve in this leadership area. Perhaps I take the idea of valuing employees for granted, and I just assume that everyone knows that treating employees poorly is a bad formula for success. I am hesitant to make any assumptions at this point because the principle of valuing employees is just too critical to understanding how Toyota successfully executes TPS.

Although I've danced around the topic of culture in previous chapters, I will now speak less about TPS and more about the values of the Toyota Way. The obvious TPS and operational excellence skills within Toyota are well known and studied, but I feel this side of the business is less understood. Nonetheless, I can assure you that the culture of Toyota described in the Toyota Way provides the good soil that allows TPS to flourish. This part of Toyota is what other companies often overlook when they try to copy Toyota's processes and equal their success.

From my past experience as a leader within Toyota, I have learned that the crucial element to valuing employees begins with building trust. No one can ever feel truly valued without first feeling a connection, a bond, and a sense of caring from their leaders. There are many ways to build trust, but for myself, I have found that nothing works better than unfailing integrity. Integrity isn't a topic that's easily broached with strangers, so this might be a good time for a little truth-telling on my part. I have no problem admitting that some people do not connect with me personally. I tend to be very direct, overly confident, and perhaps too passionate for some people. In short, these qualities can be seen by others as arrogance. I accept this notion, and I acknowledge that I do posses these characteristics. I'm not proud that some people have a difficult time connecting with me, but I am also not going to disguise my personality and pretend to be something that I am not. Integrity isn't what you know about me, it's what I know about me. There's only one person staring back in the mirror when I shave in the morning, and that's yours truly. I believe that there is a fine line between showing respect for someone with a different personality type and being false to who you are by switching your character to fit in with the dominant crowd. I just won't do this.

Here's an example of what I mean. In the past, I worked with someone who was known throughout the company as being very politically savvy. He was a great communicator, outgoing, and friendly to everyone. If asked, this person would describe almost anyone he has ever met as "a great guy." No kidding. It doesn't matter how much you know to the contrary about someone, if you asked this person he would always say, "He's a great guy." Now I'm a Christian man, and I believe in trying to find the best in everyone, but I'm also a realist. Let's face it, not everyone is "a great guy." Personally, when I can't differentiate between those who truly are "great guys" and those who are not, I begin to question the motives of the person making these assessments. It becomes a matter of integrity. I may not be as smooth and politically refined as this colleague, but people can trust that what I say reflects what I feel. At the end of the day, they can choose to agree or to disagree, but when people ask me what I think they know that my answer will reflect what I truly believe.

So who builds better trust with employees—me or this former colleague? Well, I'd say that he was definitely more well-liked, and if he were running for some kind of political office, he might have an edge with the popular vote. On the other hand, I feel that people sometimes doubted his word to some extent because everything was always seen through rose-colored glasses. I know I felt this way. When people wanted to get the "real scoop," they would come to me. People knew that I would be straight up with them, even if what I was telling them wasn't what they wanted to hear. I think, in some cases, my associate felt like he was protecting people from the truth—you know, like a parent might do with a small child. There's a time and a place for this type of leadership, but when dealing with other adults inside the workplace I feel that the best approach is straightforward honesty. People want to hear the truth, and I feel like direct honesty has helped me to build trust with my employees. Again, it hasn't won me any popularity contests, but people can always depend on me and trust that I will be truthful with them.

The last word on trust is this—it's not easy to gain, but it's really easy to lose. Building a personal connection takes time and commitment. It's only through consistency and numerous interactions that someone can truly understand your intentions and your character. Put a couple of layers of "org chart" between you and that person, and this process takes even longer. Employees at different levels within the hierarchy of a company are naturally going to have differing perspectives, opinions, and feelings. This is a normal consequence from having layers of management—people are exposed to different information and therefore they are going to perceive the company in a slightly different way. Sometimes this alone can breed some mistrust between levels of management (even when there's no specific reason for the mistrust to exist). All of these factors make building trust a difficult task that will require intentional effort on your part.

Losing trust, however, can happen in the blink of an eye. Whenever you are caught compromising the truth, the repercussions to your integrity and the trust you've built are devastating. All of the trust-building history will go right out the window. Consistency is the key, and it's always easy to be consistent when you're straightforward and honest. You'll never have to remember what you told someone when you always tell the truth. Employees will not commit to someone they do not trust. They will not trust someone who doesn't have integrity, tells half-truths, or is dishonest with people. Unless your workplace is a daycare facility or an elementary school, you're probably working with people who can handle the truth. Be consistent with your approach, be honest when sharing information, be available to your people, and never compromise your integrity for anyone. This is one way you can show your employees that they are truly valued.

Another term that has been used several times thus far in the book is *gemba*. Gemba refers to the place where work is happening. Most often, this is the place where your employees are making their daily contributions to the success of the business, and where you should visit—regularly. Your employees want to see you in gemba because they generally will not have opportunities to connect with you otherwise. Building trust or any kind of a relationship with your employees is impossible without some form of human contact.

So why is building trust with employees an essential element for managing using TPS? Although building trust with employees isn't a mutually exclusive value to Toyota, it is particularly important for companies wanting to implement TPS principles because operating within a TPS framework requires discipline and skill. When your team is performing highly skilled work with discipline, they're going to appreciate getting some recognition from management. Working by TPS principles takes a lot of effort, and your people will want to know that you understand how difficult their work really is. Sending a memo or posting a nice note of appreciation on a company message board isn't going to cut it. People want to see your face. They want to know that you are constantly seeing them following TPS, and that you recognize that this approach takes skill and discipline. They don't want you to know this because one of your second in command told you. Your employees want to see you connecting with them in the place where they work—in gemba.

I cannot stress to you enough how important this approach of management visiting gemba is within Toyota. If you're ever been inside a Toyota facility, then you know exactly what I mean. People just don't manage from behind a desk. The action is in gemba. The employees are in gemba. Your core business is happening in gemba. All of your company's opportunities (you know, the opportunities that you're deploying TPS to expose) exist in gemba. Who would want to sit behind a desk in an office somewhere when all of this is happening in gemba? It's difficult to even find a personal office in a Toyota facility—at least in one of their manufacturing facilities. The factory is the office, and there is no better way to recognize the value that your employees are bringing to your business every day than to visit them and see firsthand the contributions they are making.

Some employees might try to convince you that the best way to show that you value them is to reward them financially. Heck, I might even try to convince you of that myself. In the long run, however, the financial rewards and recognition fade away and present at best a short-term incentive for employees to perform. Eventually, most employees will discover that money does not create fulfillment or make them feel valued. Money is just too generic to build personal equity with your employees, and that's what I'm really describing here. It's like the difference between getting money for your birthday or receiving a well-thought-out gift that you've been dreaming about for months. Perhaps both gifts have the same monetary value, but the latter comes from the heart. Finding that "just right" gift for someone requires that you pay attention to the signals that person is sending. To make this personal connection with someone else, you must care more about that person and their interests than you do your own. The common, generic nature of a financial gift will not build emotional or personal equity. There's no investment of yourself or any sign of interest in the recipient when you give a generic gift. The takeaway here is that you need to understand the difference in recognition and showing value. Your people will feel valued when you invest more in them than just money—when you invest something of yourself.

Order and discipline (discipline the noun, not the verb) can also be a source of contention in the context of valuing and respecting your employees, and I believe this to be a significant topic worthy of some discussion. As you may have guessed, this is another area where I tended to deviate from the mainstream thinking within Toyota. Here's a brief history to explain my position: Born out of intimidation, TMMK's tendency was to loosen policies and procedures to avoid upsetting some team members who were vocal about wanting to form a union. Toyota has always been very clear that the decision to unionize a facility would be left up entirely to the workforce, but behind the scenes, the company was deeply concerned about the thought of what the UAW could do to their TPS and Toyota Way culture. So at TMMK to keep the peace (so to speak), many times rules and policies would be overlooked or ignored altogether by management in order to avoid possible confrontation with unhappy team members. For me, the concern wasn't happy versus unhappy, but instead consistent versus inconsistent (the latter being a huge issue when your ultimate goal is to value and respect your employees).

I've worked for a union company (Ford Motor Company), and although I personally don't feel that the team members need union representation in this day and age, I also am not fearful of working with a union. My thought is this—every organization needs some order, some structure if you will. In common practice, this order and structure manifests itself in rules, policies, and procedures. If the structure isn't necessary, then don't create it in the first place. If a rule or a policy becomes obsolete, then have practices in place to remove it. If an employee has a grievance or feels that he is being treated unfairly, then make provisions for reviewing the employee's concerns objectively. However, when it's all said and done, every organization is going to have some rules, and I believe that enforcing those rules consistently is another way that we show our employees that we value them. This comes back to the earlier comments regarding integrity. When your employees understand what is expected and you consistently uphold what you say you expect, your employees will trust you because you have shown integrity. But you cannot be consistent if there are no rules or the rules keep changing, so bringing order to the workplace is another way to show how much you value your employees.

On the union/non-union argument, I was always of the opinion that enforcing rules didn't upset employees, but changing them and being inconsistent certainly would. After all, don't all union represented employees follow rules—it's generally called a contract? Typically, employees choose to be represented by a union when they do not feel valued and respected. I always felt that the inconsistency of management posed a much greater threat for unionization, and I wasn't alone on this. So what's the learning point for you? This really isn't about unions, but instead it's about respecting your employees. Our leadership team was far from perfect on many levels, and this issue of consistently enforcing policies is one area that a more shared vision would have been beneficial for the entire organization. Consistency of top management thinking is another way that you can show your employees that they are valued and respected.

Let's face it, being a leader is not about winning a popularity contest. Some people are not going to like your methods or understand your personality. As a leader, you should make every effort to connect with your employees, but at the end of the day, you're just not going to please everyone. That's OK, and this won't stop you from executing a Lean culture in your workplace. You will, however, still need to establish consistency in how you manage your people. Even the people who don't think you're a great boss will require that you respect and value their contributions. Honestly, it's just as difficult to consistently manage and respect an employee that doesn't hold you in high regard as it is to consistently manage someone who does. In either case, the secret comes back to consistency. Consistency will develop into trust, and a relationship built on trust will evolve into feelings of respect and value by your employees.

One final thought on valuing your employees—it's OK to be wrong occasionally and to humble yourself by admitting your shortcomings to your team. It was difficult for me to get my arms around the notion that no one actually believes that I'm perfect. How did they find out? Seriously, everyone makes mistakes and bad judgments, and feeling comfortable about admitting your mistakes will build trust and emotional equity with your employees. By design, TPS will bring problems to the surface, and don't you want your employees to feel comfortable bringing those problems forward? The cycle of bringing problems forward and problem solving must be part of your culture or TPS will never take root. What better way to help stimulate the comfort of seeing problems as opportunities among your employees than to highlight some of your own shortcomings? When your people see that you are not shy about recognizing your own mistakes or problems, they too will become comfortable with bringing their problems forward. This is nothing new—it's simple lead-by-example stuff, but leading in this way will require that you make yourself somewhat vulnerable to your employees.

The real question you have to ask yourself is how badly do you want to create a culture where problems are not seen punitively but instead they are embraced as great opportunities to improve? Showing humility as a leader, embracing problems as opportunities, and taking advantage of situations to build trust with your employees may seem like mushy, feel-good management, but I've found that taking this approach will make all the difference in successfully implementing TPS. Employees who don't trust you or feel that you don't value them will not bring you their problems. This is one reason why I get so nervous when someone asks me about my experience with Lean tools but the topic of creating the right culture and leadership is not mentioned. Starting a 4S campaign or writing some standardized work is honestly the easy part of a Lean transformation. Getting the culture right is what's difficult. And if your current culture lacks some of these Toyota Way principles, such as valuing and respecting people, I just don't think your company is going to be successful implementing TPS. Instead of reading another book about conducting a successful kaizen activity, perhaps your time would be better spent reading more about the Toyota Way.

CHAPTER 8

THE PROCESS OF PROBLEM SOLVING

"If I had an hour to solve a problem, and my life depended on the solution, I would spend the first fifty-five minutes determining the proper question to ask; for once I know the proper question, I could solve the problem in less than five minutes."

—Albert Einstein

Effective problem solving is the key to sustaining continuous improvement while managing using TPS principles. As discussed previously, TPS is not made up of problem solving tools. Instead, it is a system to identify problems within the processes where TPS principles have been applied. Also, there is no "perfect" TPS. The level to which you are able to apply the TPS principles and concepts depends on many factors: the TPS skill and knowledge of the organization, the commitment level of the management team to stay true to TPS, conditions within the processes themselves, the overall stability of operations at any given time, etc. However, the more closely the concepts can be followed, and the more tightly the processes can be managed, the more effective the TPS tools will be at identifying opportunities within your processes.

The hook for most organizations undertaking a Lean transformation is the possible benefits that can be achieved through continuous improvement of their operations. After all, I realize that eventually, all of this TPS stuff must positively impact the bottom line or there isn't any justification for the effort. So what's the secret to continuous improvement? How does Toyota implement kaizen and sustain the results? Effective and sustainable kaizen cannot occur unless problem solving becomes a natural activity within your organization—a natural grassroots activity I should say. Kaizen and problem solving originate at the process and should be initiated by the people performing the work. It's these small, incremental worksite improvements that will multiply into the greater benefits that you desire, but this will take some time.

I am discovering, however, that many "would-be" TPS practitioners are struggling with the concept of kaizen at the grassroots level of their organization. Most of the companies that have been recruiting me are looking for someone who can move between their facilities and function as a "problem solving" or Lean improvement resource. Toyota also uses kaizen teams within their plants to facilitate improvement activities and as a resource for implementing kaizens, but this is not the backbone of continuous improvement and problem solving. Problem solving and the initiative for continuous improvement are the responsibility and the expectation for everyone. Have you ever heard the metaphor about feeding people fish versus teaching them to fish? Well, in the case of Toyota, the goal is to teach everyone to fish—to achieve self-reliance and eliminate interdependence on outside resources to make improvements. Sure, "giving someone a fish" works great if you're looking for a quick, stop-gap type of improvement or rapid deployment of some special initiative, but be very careful if this is your long-term approach for kaizen and problem solving. My hope is that through reading this book, you will come to see that the short-term, quick-hitting result you achieve with this approach will be difficult to sustain long term because the learning, development, and buy-in from your employees is just not there after the "special" team moves on to the next problem area.

Applying TPS principles is not complicated, and when done properly, we know that problems are going to become recognizable to the people performing the processes. Now, to make those improvements that every business desires, you will need to develop a problem solving organization. This may sound simple, but the execution of good problem solving takes as much if not more discipline than following TPS itself. Some organizations have been conditioned to believe that the best way to solve a problem is to pull together your management team in a meeting room and hash things out. I have a couple of issues with this approach. First, unless the problem exists inside a conference room, then you have no business trying to solve the problem there. Please keep in mind that

I'm referring to a problem occurring in gemba where your core work is done. Perhaps it's a bit of an oversimplification, but I'm assuming that the problem could actually be observed somewhere within your operations. Without going to see the problem firsthand, how can you be assured that the information you have is accurate? Perhaps you can understand in general terms what the problem is without going to the work site, but how will you gain a firm understanding of the conditions that created the problem? If your source of information has limited skill, knowledge, and insight regarding the potential causes of the problem, you're going to be left guessing at possible solutions. Remember, data and facts are two different things, and to effectively solve problems, you'll need the facts.

The second and more significant reason that I don't like the "conference-room" approach to solving problems is that most rooms have doors. Doors open and close for a reason—so some people can come in, and other people can be shut out. When solving a problem, the last thing you want to do is exclude "problem solvers" from your pool of possible resources. What happens to the people who are closest to the work when the problem solving starts? What kind of input and insight do the employees in the trenches have when it comes to continuously improving the work that impacts them the most? Only you can speak for the input aspect of this question, but from my experience, the insight of your employees is one of the most valuable assets that any business has. Tap into it and you'll have endless problem solving resources at your disposal. Ignore it, and you'll have the same, like-minded and often misinformed people attempting to solve problems for your company.

One way to avoid bad problem solving is to create structure in your approach—to create a process. Because Toyota's operational effectiveness is in their TPS principles and application, and because TPS makes problems visible, you can bet that Toyota has also become pretty proficient in their problem solving approach. Interestingly enough, TPS is generally not taught using what I would describe as a conventional approach. The TPS classroom is in gemba. It is taught almost exclusively through an apprenticeship type methodology where student and teacher engage in learning situations. The work area becomes the learning area, and this is where the instruction takes place (more on this later). On the other hand, Toyota approaches problem solving in a much more conventional manner. Don't get me wrong, the problem solving itself is practiced, and skills are honed in gemba, but the instruction occurs in more of a classroom setting. Problem solving is a process within Toyota with a well-defined methodology. As such, there is a definite "correct" approach that can be taught, tested, and confirmed. The thinking is—follow the process correctly, and you will always solve the problem (any problem) the first time. TPS principles, on the other hand, cannot be taught in this fashion, because there are no "defined" correct applications—only best applications for any given set of process conditions.

Another point that must be reiterated here is that in order for TPS to thrive in your company, problems must be embraced as opportunities. This has already been touched upon on several occasions, but the point bears repeating. No problem can be solved if it has been covered up and distorted beyond recognition. Sure, you might take some action to resolve the "perceived" problem, but this will not correct the deep, underlying issues that need to be addressed. And solving the wrong problem can be worse than ineffectively solving the right problem. At least in the latter case, you can take another shot at solving the problem with a different solution. When solving the wrong problem, on the other hand, you may actually be creating other issues elsewhere in your operations. For the remainder of this chapter, I will briefly describe the steps I've learned to ensure the root cause of a problem is identified and corrected every time. As stated in the introduction, this process has been included in the "hardware" section of the book to emphasize the link between applying TPS tools and good problem solving.

The first step in effective problem solving is to clearly define what problem you want to solve. As basic as this sounds, this step is overlooked all too often, and as a result, many different interpretations of the problem may develop. To avoid any confusion regarding the problem focus, step 1 is to create a general statement of fact that can be quantified and easily understood. For example: The quality level for Process A is 20% below target. Assuming that you can definitively measure the quality level and that you have a specified target, it's fair to say that this problem statement is an assertion of fact. This problem statement would then be visualized as shown in figure 8.1.

Figure 8.1   **Visualization of the Quality Problem Statement**

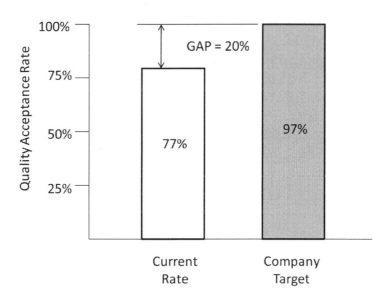

Notice that nowhere in the problem statement is there any mention of why the target is not being met. After all, we're just getting started, and this is precisely the purpose of this activity—to understand why the problem exists. To follow this process, you must never begin to solve the problem with the solution already in mind. Now, I'm sure you have some intuition and experience that can guide you in making quick problem assessments, but is it possible that your intuition is incorrect? When strictly followed, this step-by-step process will lead you to a "fact-based" solution versus a "best-guess-based-on-past-experience" solution. So in developing your problem statement, the goal is to broadly define the problem in terms of observable, measurable facts. The problem should also be stated in terms of the gap condition between your current situation and the desired goal or target.

Continuing with this quality example, it's important at this point to realize that perhaps this broad, general problem may take some time to break down and solve completely. This being the case, you may wish to consider if a "temporary" or "short-term" countermeasure is appropriate. A temporary countermeasure is taken when the consequences of the problem defined in the problem statement are not acceptable, and some immediate control must be put in place. Notice the reference to "control." The temporary countermeasure is not intended to resolve the problem, but instead its purpose is to control the consequences of the problem. Controls can take many forms, but in most cases, they involve adding resources to a process. You may be asking, "Isn't this direction contrary to TPS?" Yes, in a sense it is. This point illustrates another paradox of TPS—to reduce waste and/or excess in a process, sometimes you will need to add resources to gain temporary output control.

For example, underachievement of quality targets at Toyota was not acceptable for any reason. When normal process or operating conditions could not meet quality targets, temporary countermeasures would be put in place to protect stakeholders (the customers purchasing our products, our employees, and our sales force who relied on Toyota quality for sustained revenue and job security). Usually, the temporary countermeasure required adding more people to confirm quality and make repairs when necessary. Later, once permanent solutions were in put place based on identifying and correcting the root cause of the problem, the temporary controls would be removed.

Step 2 involves breaking down the broad problem statement into a more definitive, prioritized problem. The method used in this step is to examine the problem statement using "who," "what," "when," "where," and "how" type questions. Examples for our quality issue mentioned previously might be: What are the types of quality issues? Where are defects occurring on the vehicle? Who is causing the defects? When are the defects being created? Figure 8.2 illustrates how data would be used to visualize the answers to these types of questions.

Figure 8.2   **Visualization of the Problem Breakdown**

What types of quality issues are occurring?

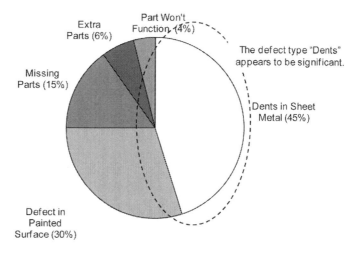

What location on the vehicle are defects occurring?

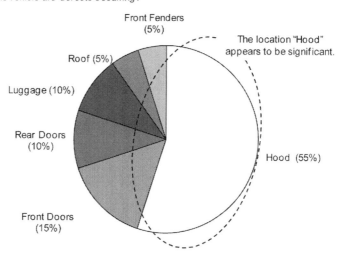

Figure 8.2 (cont) <u>**Visualization of the Problem Breakdown**</u>

Who is causing the defects?

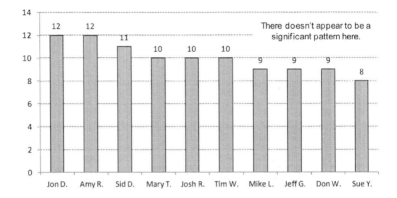

There doesn't appear to be a significant pattern here.

When are the defects being created?

Although there didn't appear to be a pattern with any particular employee, the Second Shift does seem to display a pattern for creating defects.

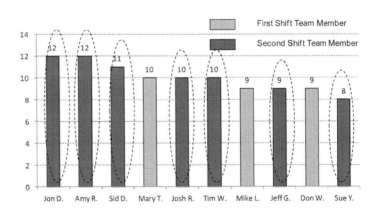

The desired outcome from this step is to identify clear patterns in the data that *factually* point to the prioritized problem. From the sample data provided in figure 8.2, there are several emerging patterns that would need to be broken down further to understand the prioritized problem. For example, is there a stronger correlation between the type of quality issue (dents) and the location on the vehicle (hood)? Perhaps the strongest correlation is related to the location on the hood regardless of the defect type, or maybe dents are the biggest problem regardless of the location. And how does the pattern of defects created on the second shift enter into the equation? Don't make any assumptions. Let the facts tell the story, and where data is inconclusive, more information should be collected to avoid possible supposition. Assumed problem identification will lead to assumed problem solving results. Conversely, however, following a disciplined problem solving process where problems are narrowed using facts will always result in effective solutions.

So why does this process emphasize identification of a prioritized problem? The broad problem defined in the problem statement will generally have multiple causes. When step 2 is followed correctly, the factors contributing most significantly to the broad problem statement will become clear (referred to as "narrowing" the problem). Although there may be some exceptions, you will tend to prioritize the factor that has the highest contribution to the problem statement. Resolving the biggest factor first (i.e., the most significant prioritized problem) will have the most favorable impact on closing the gap in your problem statement. However, let's be clear about this—in most cases, the broad problem statement cannot be resolved with a single countermeasure. Effective problem solving always requires that a broad problem be broken into smaller, prioritized problems and that each one be solved individually. So once the first prioritized problem has been resolved, you will need to return to step 2 and begin this process again with the next most significant prioritized problem. This cycle will continue until the gap condition in the problem statement (the Current Rate vs. the Target) is in an acceptable condition.

In step 3, a target should be set for improving the prioritized problem condition (note that the target for step 3 is separate from the target for the problem statement which already exists). The prioritized problem target should be challenging yet achievable and should favorably impact the overall problem statement gap identified in step 1. The main purpose for this target is to create some measurable accountability for the successful implementation of any and all countermeasures. In other words, once you've taken action to mitigate the prioritized problem, comparison of results to this target will allow you judge if the action taken was successful and to what degree. By setting a target, you are also creating an internal goal for the level of problem improvement that is acceptable. If you do not achieve this level, then you will want to consider implementing additional and/or more effective countermeasures.

The target also helps to communicate and set expectations for other stakeholders in the problem. Remember I said that team members would be a stakeholder in a quality problem? A clear, measurable target that is well communicated and understood by the team members performing the process will help ensure their buy-in and engagement in the problem solving and in the solution(s). Sharing goals and expectations throughout the organization has made a huge impact on Toyota's success with problem solving because this allows them to get buy-in from stakeholders at every step of the process. So for all general purposes, setting a target is basically the same as setting the expectations.

Step 4 is where the actual "problem solving" begins with the most basic of questions—why does the prioritized problem exist? This is the first time any question beginning with "why" should be asked. Remember, during step 2 we were asking "who," "what," "when," "where," and "how" types of questions to break the general problem statement into a more defined prioritized problem. Never during that process, however, should "why" questions be asked because these are cause-finding questions versus condition-finding questions. Step 4 is the time to start identifying causes for the narrowed prioritized problem. There are several handy tools that can and should be used here to organize your problem solving. The two that I have found to be the most effective are the 4M Fishbone Diagram and the 5-Whys. In applying these tools, however, remember what I discussed earlier in the book about solving problems in gemba versus in a conference room. There is no substitute for going and seeing the problem firsthand.

The 4Ms of the 4M Fishbone Diagram stand for man (or human if you like that better), method, machine, and material. Sometimes a fifth "M," for management, is added to this analysis. The term *fishbone* is in reference to the visual form of the diagram which looks similar to the skeleton of a fish. The

4M analysis is completed by considering all of the potential contributing factors that fall within the broad category of each one of the Ms. Building on this quality problem for example, in the machine category, one might conclude that improper calibration of the equipment could contribute to a quality problem. Other possible factors might include poor maintenance, equipment idling or downtime, and improper use of or misapplication of the equipment. Refer to figure 8.3 for an example of a possible 4M Fishbone Diagram for solving our fictitious quality problem.

Figure 8.3   Example of Fishbone Diagram Using the 4Ms

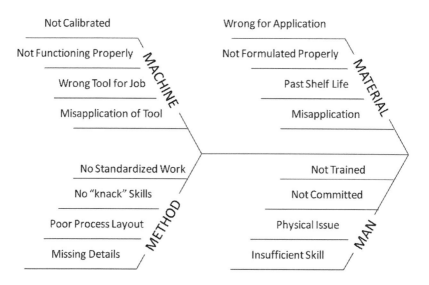

The depth of information presented in the 4M Fishbone Diagram is limited only by the specifics of the problem, the number of failure modes for the process, and the skill and knowledge of the person(s) performing the analysis. The final point here requires a little further explanation. In order to complete a 4M Fishbone Diagram that accurately represents all of the potential failure and risk points that may be contributing to the prioritized problem, the individual(s) performing the failure mode assessment must be highly informed, skilled, and knowledgeable about the process. Basically, you'll never find the actual cause of the prioritized problem if you cannot first identify a complete list of the potential causes. This is specifically why you'll want your grassroots process owners involved in the problem solving activities. They will have knowledge and insight about the process that no one else will have. Also, this is where the true root cause of the problem will begin to surface, so having that trust factor that problems are seen as opportunities is critical to the successful completion of this step.

Once the 4M Fishbone Diagram has been completed for each of the 4Ms, it's time to start confirming which elements are being controlled and which ones are out of control. This must be done with reliable data or by some other quantifiable means. What you don't want to do here is use opinions and highly subjective analysis to rule out any of these potential failure and risk points. If, however, you can prove factually that a risk factor is not contributing to the problem, then simply cross that item off the Fishbone and move on to the next possible cause. Here are some examples of what you might consider analytic proof:

1) You can produce records of preventative maintenance and standardized work that indicate that the equipment has been calibrated correctly.
2) The equipment has electronic data logging capability that can be tracked and confirmed for accuracy and calibration compliance.
3) Your equipment's downtime history is logged automatically, and there is no link between any downtime of the equipment and any quality issues.

The following would not be considered analytical proof and should not be used to disqualify any potential risk factor:

1) You spoke with a supervisor in the area and he assured you that the equipment is being calibrated.
2) No one working in this process can remember any recent equipment downtime.
3) Even though no written standards exist for the equipment maintenance, you're told that everyone who works on the equipment basically knows what he is doing.

When there is no quantifiable method to confirm or disprove that one of the Fishbone risk factors is contributing to the prioritized problem, then I would suggest that you take the "guilty-until-proven-innocent" approach. Essentially, if there is a risk factor for the process that cannot be proven to be in control, assume that it is out of control. To avoid this concern in the future, you might want to consider adding some monitoring method to ensure process control traceability. If you aren't familiar with how to achieve this, I would suggest adding some SPC (statistical process control) expertise to your team's set of skills. You will also need these skills to sustain improvements once your problem areas have been mitigated.

The 5-Whys method should be used in conjunction with (not separate from) the 4M Fishbone Diagram. All risk factors that have been identified as "not controlled" can be drilled into further by asking the question "why" five times. Here's an example of applying the 5-Whys method: Let's assume for the purpose of this example that "MACHINE—Not Calibrated" is determined to be a contributing risk factor to the problem. Therefore, the 5-Whys analysis for this risk factor might look as follows:

> *Contributing factor.* The machine is not being calibrated.
> Why (1) Because the machine is running around the clock.
> Why (2) Because the production rate cannot be achieved.
> Why (3) Because the scrap rate for this process is above target.
> Why (4) Because parts are scrapped due to incorrect loading.
> Why (5) Because untrained operators are performing the process.

By asking the question "why" five times, we can see that the untrained operators performing the process is the root cause for "The Machine is not being calibrated." But wouldn't the fact that untrained operators are performing the process show up somewhere else in the Fishbone analysis—say under MAN or possibly METHOD? Perhaps, but let's not forget that when we were evaluating man (operator) and method (standardized work) failure modes, we were looking for connections to a specific prioritized problem. Based on applying the 5-Whys method, you now know that the untrained operators were creating scrap, a different problem that may have been hidden from the original quality issue. The scrap may have been detected and removed from the process by the operator, but the operator didn't identify that scrap was causing other issues as well. The effect of the equipment not being calibrated, however, may have manifested itself somewhere else in the process—somewhere not detectable by the operator.

This is why good problem solving requires deep analysis—to ask "why" five times if you will. For instance, in this example, if you stopped asking "why" after only the first or the second time, you might conclude that adding more equipment capacity to the process would be an effective countermeasure. The additional capacity might come from speeding up the existing equipment, or heaven forbid, even purchasing some additional equipment. Neither of these countermeasures would address the root cause of ineffective new operator training. The scrap rates would stay high, and even if the additional equipment capacity did create enough time in your production schedule to complete the calibrations, you would still be faced with the waste of the scrap in the process. Asking "why" five times creates a discipline for looking below the surface and beyond the obvious.

In step 5, countermeasures or corrective actions will be developed for the root causes of the problem identified in step 4. This is a great time for innovation and creativity and a time when careful consideration must be taken to gauge the effectiveness of every possible solution. As countermeasures are considered, ask yourself the following questions: Can this solution be sustained over time? Is it practical to implement or would new technology be required? How much would this solution cost—including both the initial investment and the ongoing operating costs? Can the countermeasure be implemented without having an adverse impact on other aspects of the business—safety, productivity, or other quality issues? The matrix shown in figure 8.4 is a good tool for comparing the effectiveness of different countermeasures.

Figure 8.4   **Countermeasure Comparison Matrix**

Countermeasure Idea	Decision Criteria						
	Safety Impact	Feasibility To Implement	Investment Cost	Operating Cost	Employee Morale	Flexibility for Future Operations	Total Rating
Countermeasure A	0	-1	-1	1	1	0	0
Countermeasure B	1	-1	0	2	0	2	4
Countermeasure C	0	0	-1	0	0	0	-1
Countermeasure D	0	1	-2	2	2	1	4
Countermeasure E	1	1	-2	-1	2	1	2

Matrix Scoring: -2 - Very Poor/ Negative   -1 – Poor/ Negative   0 - Neutral   1 - Good/ Positive   2 - Very Good/ Positive

Based on the scoring system and the decision criteria used in this matrix, Countermeasures B and D would have the most favorable overall impact to operations. Does this mean that both countermeasures should be implemented? Perhaps, but if cash on hand is currently scarce, Countermeasure D might not be the first choice even though overall it ranks equally with Countermeasure B (i.e., because the "Investment Cost" ranking is -2: Very Poor/Negative). If on the other hand, employee morale is a sensitive issue at your company, you may want to choose implementation of Countermeasure D because this option scores very highly in the "Employee Morale" category. Although the decision criteria in the matrix used in this example was weighted equally, the weighting can be changed based on your particular business priorities at any given time. One side note concerning this type of matrix is that it can be very useful for comparing all sorts of decisions and options. I have used them to help my children compare colleges, to select a new home, and even to decide if I should continue on a certain career path. Perhaps this method isn't completely quantitative, but if the decision criteria is evaluated with equal objectivity for each countermeasure, the best relative option should become apparent.

Once you've evaluated your countermeasures (based on whatever criteria you believe to be the most relevant), it's time to develop a countermeasure implementation plan—step 6. You might be tempted to overlook or underestimate the importance of this step, but I would caution you against this. Here's why—in most cases when following this process for problem solving, I have found that there are multiple potential root causes for your prioritized problem. This isn't the end of the world, but what it does mean is that you should systematically implement countermeasures in order to accurately judge the individual impact each countermeasure contributes. If you decide to implement everything at once, you may never know which countermeasure had the most significant impact (and trust me, one or two of them will be more significant than the rest). Additionally, if your countermeasures are going to involve committing resources such as time and money, you may not want to implement Countermeasure B if after implementing Countermeasure D, 95% of the original problem is corrected. This is another great argument for taking the temporary or short-term countermeasure that we discussed toward the beginning of this chapter. An effective short-term countermeasure should be controlling the problem, which in turn buys you some time to be more strategic with your permanent countermeasure implementation.

Step 7—Once you've identified a root cause, determined a good countermeasure, and have a plan, it's time to get that countermeasure implemented. By now, you may be too exhausted to implement a countermeasure, but hang in there because we're almost done! When I first began practicing this method of problem solving I must admit that I too became exhausted from this seemingly endless process. But step 7 embodies the most redeeming qualities of the entire process. When the proper attention to detail is applied to the first six steps (which I will admit do take a fair amount of time and discipline to complete) you will ultimately save time and resources when implementing your solutions. You'll be more efficient at this point because you have spent your time and effort wisely preparing for the solution that you're about to deploy. You have done your homework. The countermeasure you're about to implement has been proven to address the root cause of the prioritized problem which means you shouldn't have to deal with this same problem ever again. Based on the quote I included at the beginning of this chapter, I'd say Mr. Einstein also agreed with this concept.

Conversely, if you enter into a problem solving activity with shallow information, no facts, and opinion-driven solutions with no buy-in from your stakeholders, chances are pretty good that even though you might be able to proceed at a good pace, you're going to be right back where you started in just a short time. What Toyota has developed is a process to find and solve the right problem the first time. Yes, it does take time (and most of all, discipline), but the results are sustainable. The "whack-a-mole" approach to problem solving will drain an organization of all of its strength and resources, destroy motivation, and it will not support your efforts to implement TPS. Again, if you want to successfully deploy TPS which is basically a system for identifying problems, your organization better become proficient at problem solving.

On to the eighth and final step—sustain and transfer your countermeasures to other applicable areas. First let's talk about sustainment. After your countermeasure has been implemented and the process is stable, you'll need to check the actual versus target performance indicators for the prioritized problem. Did the gap close as you had predicted? If not, what are your follow-up plans? If the gap did close, are your results repeatable? The key point here is that you continue checking your actual results versus your target, and make adjustments using a P–D–C–A cycle described in chapter 6.

Transferring a countermeasure (or *yokoten* in Toyota language) is a great way to parlay your problem solving into additional benefits for your company. After all, if the countermeasures taken effectively solved one problem, they might just be beneficial in other areas as well. The problem solving "work" has already been done, and your results are proven, so why not invest these great problem solving efforts elsewhere? Perhaps your business has multiple facilities performing similar processes that could benefit from one site's solutions? This is how good organizations become great organizations—they take full advantage of every opportunity, leaving nothing on the table. Your resources are just too valuable, and no organization can afford to waste time solving the same problems over and over again.

The problem solving process described in this chapter is tedious and it will take time to master. Don't think that because you've read these few pages that you're now ready to be proficient using this technique. Honestly, I'm not sure if such a person exists—even in Toyota. What I can tell you is this—the more you practice using this method of problem solving, the more intuitive it will become, and eventually, the process will become more natural and efficient. You'll need commitment and perseverance to use this approach. However, if you do not practice problem solving regularly by following these steps completely and in the prescribed order, this method is only going to frustrate you.

Regardless of the approach you take, I would recommend that your organization become proficient at problem solving because there will be no shortage of problems (or more positively stated—opportunities) in an organization properly applying Lean tools. This is Toyota's fundamental reason for using TPS to manage—to effectively highlight and solve problems.

CHAPTER 9

PROCESS MEASUREMENT FOR IMPROVEMENT

You cannot improve what you do not measure. The practical application of kaizen is really that simple, and process measurement will provide you with the information needed for continuous improvement and problem solving. Consider these questions: How will you recognize where your business's opportunities are without measuring process performance? How will you judge your business's capability to meet objectives? Once you've kaizened a process, how will you know if the results have improved or worsened? The answer to all of these questions is—you're going to need some process measurements to understand how your business is performing. If you have no process measurements now, you're flying blind. Sure, you may have some company level metrics that explain the basic operating conditions of the business, but this level is too far removed to understand the incremental impact that every process is having on your bottom line. Yes, every process and, therefore, every employee impacts your bottom line, and this is the level where TPS can help you make significant improvements in your operations.

In this chapter, we will explore the definition and concept of key performance indicators (or KPIs). KPIs are the measurement standards used to judge conditions within any process and to measure all facets of the business—safety, quality, cost, productivity, throughput, on time delivery rates, etc. Generally, KPIs are divided into two types—Result KPIs and Process KPIs. Result KPIs are defined as the measurement of the final, cumulative output of all the processes at the company level. So if we use safety as an example, a typical Results KPI used in industry is OSHA Case Rate or OSHA Incident Rate (a standard developed by the Bureau of Labor Statistics to compare relative levels of injuries and illnesses among industries). For example, if the

OSHA Case Rate for a particular facility was 7.5, this would indicate that over the course of one year 7.5% of the workforce would experience a qualified OSHA injury or illness. This number represents the results or a final outcome of the safety conditions for a facility, but what does this really tell you about this company's safety practices? Well, if you knew the OSHA Case Rate from other facilities you could compare the relative "safeness" of the companies. Similarly, if you had a history of the Case Rate for any individual facility (say for the past ten years), you could assess the overall injury rate trend over that period. A Results KPI such as the OSHA Case Rate is very difficult to use for anything other than a broad diagnosis or visualization of a condition.

Process KPIs, on the other hand, are used specifically to measure process activity. Still using the safety example, perhaps this same hypothetical facility having an OSHA Case Rate of 7.5 also uses a safety auditing tool to observe safe practices. Typically, these tools would have a list of criteria which could be used to judge employee compliance to safety standards and/or best practices. Examples of such criteria might include: Are employees wearing safety glasses properly? Are employees complying with pedestrian safety rules? Are employees rushing? Are employees paying attention to the work they are performing ("eyes on task")? By conducting audits and observing many workers, data can be compiled and analyzed to understand what types of "at risk behaviors" exist in the facility.

For the Process KPI example of safety auditing, let's assume that only 85% of the employees are wearing their safety glasses properly. From this data, one could deduce that 15% of the employees are "at risk" for an eye injury due to not wearing their protective equipment. This is a Process KPI. These observed behaviors have not necessarily resulted in an injury that would be reported in the OSHA Case Rate (the Results KPI), but they do provide some indication of the safety culture, practices, and processes within the facility. Understanding these factors "analytically" versus "subjectively" is crucial for solving problems and questioning the current condition of your TPS standards.

The successful deployment of TPS requires the proficient use of Process KPIs because this is where people are performing the core work of the business. The measurement of every process may seem overwhelming at the higher levels in the organization, and it should. Process KPIs are not meant to be used by upper management for problem solving, but by the process owners. These are the people who need to understand the capability of the processes they are performing daily. That doesn't mean that senior management won't need to know or shouldn't know what is happening with their employees. Everyone should have the ability to see what is happening in gemba, but when Process KPIs are being measured sufficiently, the amount of detail is much more than most management will be able to use effectively (at least on a daily basis for managing operations).

So once process measurement has been established, how will you judge what is acceptable and what must be improved? To make sense of this, we should refer to the concept of "Shared Vision and Direction" from chapter 4. Direction must be set by leadership and should be shared throughout all levels of the organization. One way of sharing the direction is by setting targets for high-level Results KPIs that can be broken down further into Process KPIs. These targets then become the standard process performance requirements and can be used to set goals for each employee throughout the organization.

Continuing with the safety example mentioned previously, let's imagine that the president of a small company has the vision of becoming the safest manufacturer in his particular industry. After researching and comparing similar companies, the president finds that a 2.5 OSHA Case Rate would be "Best-in-Class" for safety performance. He sets this rate as the company's goal and then communicates it throughout the organization. Every employee supports the idea of working in a safe environment, and therefore, they share the president's vision.

So what would this high lever Results KPI look like at a process level? What would individual workers do to contribute to the achievement of this company wide Results KPI target? Here's one possible approach. With a little research you could discover a simple model called "Heinrich's Pyramid" (see figure 9.1). First discussed in 1931 in H.W. Heinrich's book *Industrial Accident Prevention*, this model shows the statistical relationship between unsafe acts (called "Near Miss Incidents"), first-aid type injuries (called "Minor Injuries"), and OSHA qualified injuries (called "Major Injuries"). Most safety specialists are familiar with this research. The validity of this model is constantly being challenged, but many people (including me) still believe that Heinrich's theory can be used as a predictor of how behaviors impact injury rates.

Figure 9.1   **Heinrich's Pyramid**

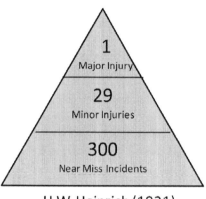

H.W. Heinrich (1931)

The president has given the company's Results KPI for OSHA Case Rate, but you'll need to do some simple calculations and then apply the theory behind Heinrich's Pyramid to create a Process KPI that frontline employees can manage. To calculate the equivalent number of "Major Injuries" that will result in an OSHA Case Rate of 2.5, we must refer to the following standard equation used by OSHA to calculate Case Rate:

$$\frac{\text{Total \# of Injuries} \times 200,000}{\text{Total Hours worked by all employees}} = \text{OSHA Case Rate}$$

By manipulating this equation and then adding some additional information about the fictitious workforce (i.e., the company has 200 employees and the employees work 40 hours per week), we can solve for the total number of injuries (or "Major Injuries" from Heinrich's Pyramid) that will achieve the targeted Case Rate the president has given as the company's goal:

$$\text{Total \# of Injuries} = \frac{\text{OSHA Case Rate} \times \text{Total Hours worked by all employees}}{200,000}$$

$$\text{Total \# of Injuries} = \frac{2.5\ (200\ \text{people} \times 40\ \text{hr/wk} \times 52\ \text{wks})}{200{,}000} = 5\ \text{Injuries}$$

According to the OSHA calculation the number of Major Injuries the company can have and still achieve the president's goal is approximately five injuries—still the top number in the pyramid. By applying the ratio of Near Misses (300) to Major Injuries (1) from Heinrich's Pyramid, you will arrive at a final number of 1500 Near Misses. Keeping in mind that this is a statistical model and not an exact science, you may choose to throw in a safety factor to allow for some wiggle room in the Process KPI. Maybe the target should be set somewhere in the 1200 to 1400 Near Miss range to create reasonable confidence that the organization will not exceed the company's goal of a 2.5 OSHA Case Rate.

Therefore, at the grassroots level of the organization, you decide to create a Process KPI target of less than 1200 Near Misses observed during safety audits. Statistically, if the employees can minimize the Near Misses or "unsafe acts" on the floor to less than 1200 in a year, the company should have a reasonably good chance of meeting the target of Best-in-Class safety with an OSHA Case Rate of less than 2.5. By breaking the company's Result KPI target into a Process KPI target, you will be providing more clarity, meaning, and relevance to your employees at the working level—the level where the core work is done and where your safety practices are managed using standardized work for each process.

Now I understand that there are other factors involved in the Case Rate and what qualifies as a "recordable injury" per the OSHA standards. That's not the point. I am merely trying to illustrate a simple method for setting a Process KPI target that logically rolls up into a Results KPI target. Don't get too hung up on the methodology here. The fact is that you cannot manage the Results target at the floor level—it's just too abstract and far removed from the work being done at the process. However, your employees will be able to relate to the "unsafe acts" which are being measured, and this is what they can manage and control by themselves. The work done on the floor is defined by standardized work, and therefore, the Process KPIs are really a measurement of how well TPS is being followed in each process.

We've looked at a few examples of Results and Process KPIs, and it's time to discuss how these indicators can be used practically to manage your operations. In chapter 8, we reviewed the process used by Toyota for problem solving, and this is exactly where KPIs are going to come into play. During step 1 of this process, the Problem Statement is created. This is where the Results KPI will be used. Remember, this statement is the high-level, general description of the problem. Let's consider reversing the safety scenario we've been using. What if the company wasn't achieving the target given by the president and the current OSHA Case Rate was 3.4? The Problem Statement would be: The company's OSHA Case Rate is 0.9 above the target of 2.5. The visualization of the Problem Statement is shown in figure 9.2.

Figure 9.2   **Visualization of Problem Statement**

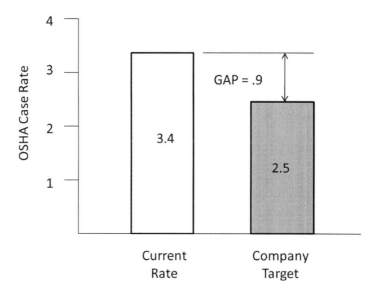

When breaking the problem down in step 2, you would eventually expect to see a correlation between Results and Process KPIs. What are the Process KPIs for safety? What types of injuries are occurring? When are they occurring? Where are they occurring? Who is having these injuries? The objective is to narrow the focus of the general Problem Statement into something that can be observed, measured, and ultimately corrected at the process level. A sample of the problem breakdown is shown on the following page. Again, in a true or "real world" scenario, the problem breakdown would be completed with actual Process KPI data. Also, as we discussed in chapter 8, you can't work backward from a problem and manipulate the facts to support a predetermined solution. The data "is what it is" and must be used factually, not hypothetically. In this case I've created some data to help visualize how the Process KPI should roll up and impact the Results KPI of the Problem Statement.

The 3.4 OSHA Case Rate is equivalent to seven injuries (a number that you would already know because, presumably, you would be calculating and tracking your Case Rate at some regular frequency—say monthly). In this example, the injuries have been broken down into cumulative (repetitive motion type injuries occurring over longer periods of time) and acute injuries (those that occur instantly and generally have a known mechanism for the injury). From the safety Process KPIs that are already being tracked, it is apparent that most of the injuries are acute. Using more detailed acute injury Process KPI data, the trend toward eye injuries stands out. Further data breakdown indicates no pattern for the point of occurrence by section, but when broken down by shift, it is obvious that all of the eye injuries have occurred on the night shift—a pattern which certainly seems significant. Finally, the Process KPI data from the night shift safety audit shows a significant number of "safety glasses" issues which supports the acute eye injury data.

But is the data from the safety audit really a Process KPI? After all, isn't this an "internal" method used to understand injury risk? If this isn't an "official" safety calculation used by OHSA and other industries, how can the data be validated? As you will find, most Process KPIs are specific to your individual processes and are not industry standards. In short, the Process KPIs are developed internally to give you the information you need to manage each process. There are no specific rules for Process KPIs, but I would consider using these guidelines: First, Process KPIs should be significant to the employee(s) performing the work that is being measured. After all, the purpose of the Process KPI is to bring meaning to their work and clarify their goals and targets. Second, regardless of how you define the Process KPI, the data must be used to manage the process. Collecting data and not using it is a waste of time and will send mixed messages about goal achievement to your employees. We'll discuss this issue at more length in the next chapter on Shop Floor Management.

Sample Date for OSHA Case Rate Problem Breakdown

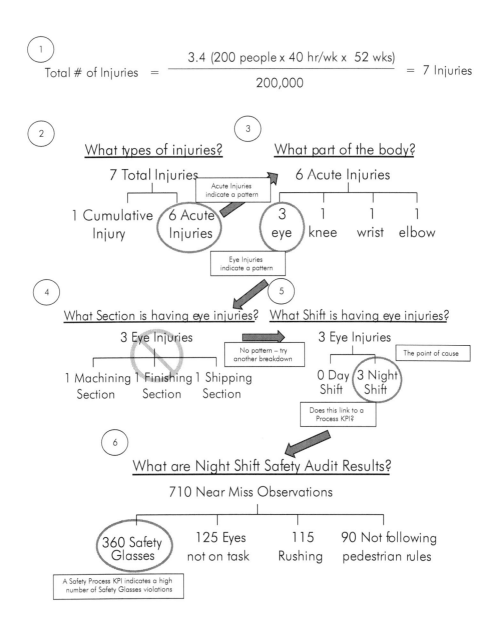

1

$$\text{Total \# of Injuries} = \frac{3.4 \ (200 \text{ people} \times 40 \text{ hr/wk} \times 52 \text{ wks})}{200,000} = 7 \text{ Injuries}$$

2   **3**

What types of injuries?   What part of the body?

7 Total Injuries   6 Acute Injuries

Acute Injuries indicate a pattern

1 Cumulative Injury   6 Acute Injuries   3 eye   1 knee   1 wrist   1 elbow

Eye Injuries indicate a pattern

4   **5**

What Section is having eye injuries?   What Shift is having eye injuries?

3 Eye Injuries   3 Eye Injuries

No pattern – try another breakdown

The point of cause

1 Machining Section   1 Finishing Section   1 Shipping Section   0 Day Shift   3 Night Shift

Does this link to a Process KPI?

6

What are Night Shift Safety Audit Results?

710 Near Miss Observations

360 Safety Glasses   125 Eyes not on task   115 Rushing   90 Not following pedestrian rules

A Safety Process KPI indicates a high number of Safety Glasses violations

At this point, I can feel some of your skepticism, but believe me when I tell you that facts don't lie. In most cases your Process KPIs are going to roll right up to the Results KPIs just as I've shown here. If they don't, chances are that you aren't measuring the significant performance aspects of your processes. In other words, the results don't happen by accident. Every result occurs for specific reasons—reasons that you can and you should control. If not, then you're leaving your business's success up to fate. The tracking and visualization of Process KPIs will give you data to help you break down and understand your results.

Another huge benefit of tracking and visualizing Process KPIs that are linked to your overall Results KPI targets is that your company will transform from having a handful of managers into a company with many managers. What do I mean by this? When you have a workforce that understands your company's direction, and they can track their own performance to support goals using Process KPIs and targets, all of your employees will be managing the business. Sure, everyone is managing at different levels, but honestly, this should be exactly what you desire—people managing what they have the ability, authority, alignment, and the accountability to control.

Perhaps you can even extrapolate to a future when Process KPIs become one of the tools for creating accountability and/or acknowledgement in your organization. Many businesses already have processes for tying company performance with employee pay. When the company performance metric is a Results KPI, many of the employees will become discouraged because they cannot see how their contributions impact the larger company KPI. On the other hand, when using Process KPIs to measure performance, your employees will see a direct connection between their effort and the net impact to the company's results.

This chapter has many links and overlaps several other subjects discussed within this book—shop floor management, employee engagement, problem solving, shared vision and direction, etc. The bottom line is this—you cannot improve what you do not measure. TPS is about continuous improvement and problem solving. Ultimately, however, my management teachings are also about engaging employees and creating meaningful work. People want to know they are making a difference. They want to understand how the work they are performing adds to the value of their company. All of these reasons support the need for measuring processes, and it's been my experience that this is one of the biggest gaps for businesses today. If you want to get on track and make some dramatic improvements to your operations, consider how you can deploy better process measurement into the daily work of your employees.

CHAPTER 10

BRING ORDER TO TPS THROUGH SHOP FLOOR MANAGEMENT

Shop floor management (SFM) is the process used in gemba to align employees with business objectives, drive continuous improvement, and sustain management activity through the P–D–C–A cycle. My best analogy to explain SFM goes something like this: Consider that a carpenter's goal is to build a house. Imagine that each TPS tool is like a tool in the carpenter's belt. SFM would then be similar to the blueprint the carpenter uses to build the house with the individual tools.

For many years, Toyota itself struggled with deploying a system for managing the production operations at their transplant facilities outside of Japan. What they eventually learned was that SFM is not always intuitive for the group leaders (Toyota's position for the frontline supervisor, abbreviated GL). While it can be learned tacitly, a better method to develop the SFM skills of the GL is to teach a standardized process. So that's precisely what happened within Toyota, and the process of SFM was created. Some of the most experienced manufacturing leaders from within TMC collaborated to adopt what they believed to be the very best work standards within Toyota for managing the shop floor. In fact, so much time and effort has gone into the development of SFM that an entirely new division within Toyota was created to support its deployment globally. It should go without saying, but the methodology of SFM encompasses all of the basic theories and philosophies of TPS and the Toyota Way and bundles them into a standard operating procedure for the frontline supervisors.

What does this process of SFM look like? Essentially it consists of three core elements:

1. Visual management/4S
2. KPI measurement, visualization, and management
3. Change point management or CPM

Until approximately eight years ago, none of the Toyota facilities were managing these business elements similarly. Now, the SFM process has been standardized and is being practiced in all Toyota facilities worldwide, and it is audited by TMC for consistency on a routine basis. Why is this significant? SFM is how Toyota wants each of their individual facilities to manage using TPS, and as a rule of thumb Toyota will "inspect" what they "expect"—part of the "check" from the P–D–C–A cycle discussed in chapter 6.

Some of the standard practices for good SFM have already been discussed, but it makes sense to highlight them here as well—at least in the context of how they fit into the SFM process. In previous chapters, the concept of gemba has been mentioned numerous times. Going to gemba is a consistent theme that is applicable to many aspects of managing a TPS organization, but here in SFM the relevance is particularly significant. The hardline Toyota concept is that you cannot manage your core business from anywhere other than where it occurs. If your business is in sales, then you need to visit your retail outlets and understand what your sales associates are experiencing every day. You need to see and hear your customers. If you own a small trucking company, you need to ride along with one of your drivers every once in a while and keep the "road experience" fresh in your mind. Regardless of what type of business you manage, in order to achieve the best results, you'll need to spend plenty of time in gemba to understand the current condition of your core business.

SFM also requires considerable effort from your workforce—especially the GL. The effort I'm talking about won't be directly linked to the products you produce or the services you provide. The SFM process is targeted primarily at the administration and strategic side of the business and therefore does not directly impact the operations. Indirectly, however, SFM provides the structure by which all operational decisions are made. When Toyota first introduced this process in their facilities, the GLs who had been managing for years were quite upset because of the additional work required to follow this new process. Using SFM standards meant that specific KPIs had to be kept up to date and displayed to ensure good visibility of the progress toward achieving targets. In the beginning, the "administrative" portion of managing using SFM took hours of a GL's daily time. This time is used to track and trend KPIs and to initiate and follow up on individual problem solving activities within their group. Because of the standard approach and requirements specified by SFM, many of Toyota's GLs felt that they were losing their autonomy to manage. Eventually, this became less and less of an issue, but initially, the resistance from the GLs to manage using SFM was very significant. This may be a good learning point for those of you considering a similar approach at your company. We'll speak more about frontline supervision in the next chapter, but in this chapter, you'll want to pay particular attention to how the SFM process adds burden to their job.

Visual Management

In chapter 2, several core TPS concepts were discussed including visual management. This is the first element of SFM because Toyota believes that nothing can be managed until the actual conditions are clearly understood. You may be wondering, "which actual conditions?" Well, in short, everything about the process. When I say visual I don't just mean "visible to the eye," but more specifically I mean "perceptible by the mind's eye." Visual management goes beyond the sense of sight to include all senses—sensory management if you will. The purpose of visual management is to quickly and easily determine if the current conditions of a process meet the standard conditions. Good visual management will also help you to determine if the current process standards are sufficient to support daily operations.

Here's a quick example: Let's say that you work in a restaurant and the first task you do when you get to work is take inventory of the food pantry. Because you have worked at this particular restaurant for years, you know how much food you can expect to use on any given night. One day, you take some much-needed time off, and upon returning, you learn that the previous evening there were several customers' orders that could not be filled because the pantry was emptied of some ingredients. You're confident that you would have caught this problem had you been at work the previous day, but the person who filled in was less experienced and missed the inventory shortage. So what's the solution? Perhaps it's more training for the person who missed the inventory shortage. If the stock information can be standardized and taught, then this might be an acceptable approach, but what if some of the current usage information is intuitive and not easily documented? How do you capture years of experience into training, and how many people would need to be trained? What would happen to the training solution if the menu were to change?

Perhaps instead of training more employees, the solution to the inventory management problem is to make the required stock quantities more visual. For example, the positions for the entire food inventory on the shelves should be standardized and labeled. There may be some good logic as to how the food is grouped on the shelves as well—condiments, canned foods, fresh foods, etc. all stored together in a similar location. The lighting in the pantry should be measured to ensure that all of the food items can be clearly seen and counted if necessary. Common items with high usage should be placed in the most accessible and visible area on the shelving to make inventory taking more simple. Clear signage to indicate standard and min/max stock conditions will also help when determining reorder quantities. Another solution might be to incorporate a kanban system (a signal to reorder) to ensure that every food item is accounted for at the time that it is used. Implementing a kanban system would virtually eliminate the need for taking inventory altogether, or at a minimum decrease the inventory frequency considerably.

The improvements listed above would hardly make sense for the "expert" who has taken inventory for years. He already knows this stuff, so why take the extra time to add this additional detail? Visual management eliminates the need for experts who are, after all, hard to come by. Developing experts takes lots of time and resources, and when they aren't around, who is capable to step up and do their work? By adding the visual management as suggested in the food pantry example, we can, in theory, make anyone an expert. With some simple training on how to read the signage and fill out an order form, we should be able to teach anyone how to quickly and reliably take the inventory. The more visual the system is, the less time it will take—even for the folks with little to no previous experience. And let's face it, taking inventory isn't making the restaurant any money, but running out of food is certainly costing the business from a lost revenue standpoint (not to mention having a negative impact on customer satisfaction with their dining experience). A quicker inventory process or elimination of inventory taking entirely will save money, and an accurate inventory method will ensure that customers are able to dine on the menu item of their choice.

The concept of visual management is simple, and the opportunities to apply it in the workplace are limitless. The hang-up most businesses run into when making the workplace more visual is that they only ask their experts how to make improvements. But as we just discussed, is the visual management for the experts? What kind of ideas are you going to get from people who already know what they're doing? They will probably miss many important details because their familiarity with the job is blinding them. Actually, one of the best times to implement or improve the visual management of a process is when a new employee is being trained. Those with the least experience will tend to ask the most probing and insightful questions as they are learning. The answers to these questions can be simplified by challenging both the trainer and the new employee to think in terms of visual management.

One final benefit from implementing an improved visual management system is that abnormal conditions will become that much more apparent to everyone. The more visual the process is, the easier it will be for anyone to differentiate an abnormal condition from a normal one. When a method such as a "shadow board" for hand tools is used (see figure 10.1 on the following page), anyone walking past the tool storage area can recognize if one of the required tools is missing and quick action can be taken. If all of the same tools were thrown in a drawer somewhere, no one would ever see them. More importantly, no one would understand what is needed, what is present currently, and what is missing. On a related note, consider how this shadow board could be even more visually effective if the tools were not shown as solid black silhouettes but instead were shown only as an outline—perhaps even a red outline. As the board exists in the current condition, someone might mistake a solid black shadow for the tool itself, but even from a distance, a red outline could be differentiated from an actual tool.

Figure 10.1   **Simple Example of a Hand Tool Shadow Board**

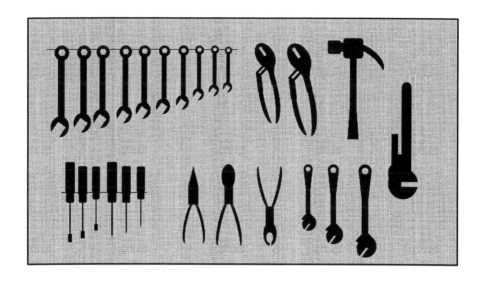

KPI Measurement, Visualization, and Management

The second element of SFM is KPI measurement, visualization, and management. On the shop floor, you can bet that the KPIs we're going to be concerned about are Process KPIs. We've already discussed KPIs in chapter 9, so we're not going to spend any more time talking about KPI measurement. What we do need to think about, however, is KPI visualization and management. What does it mean to visualize a KPI? Am I suggesting that we somehow train employees to imagine a KPI being achieved so they will be motivated to meet their goals? Although this might have some psychological significance, that's not what I mean by visualizing KPIs. What I'm talking about in this case is literally making Process KPIs visible to employees. This can be done in several ways, but the simplest is to dedicate some floor space for displaying your significant Process KPIs on a communication board. This method tends to work well for shared Process KPIs that can be reviewed with your employees frequently in a group setting. The reason for an open display or board is to ensure accessibility to everyone and at anytime. Information that is hidden in a desk or on someone's computer doesn't meet the criteria for visualization, and as we'll discuss momentarily, these KPIs are probably also not being managed.

So the benefit of making the Process KPIs visual is that all concerned parties can now stay informed and make informed assessments regarding the condition of their process. Remember that process kaizen should ideally originate with the employees performing the work, so when each employee can gauge for himself how his process is performing, the need for kaizen becomes readily apparent. Reviewing Process KPIs is one method used to engage employees quickly and without having to rally the team with a pep talk when goals aren't being met. Your team can see for themselves every day if their process targets are being achieved. For instance, when quality numbers are below target or scrap is over goal, all the process owner has to do is look at his KPIs to understand the opportunity for improvement. How much are the results over target? How long has the target been missed? Is there a pattern for when the target is made or missed? Hopefully, you can imagine how having Process KPI data available at the level of the process owners makes problem identification and breakdown much simpler.

This gets us into the final portion of the KPI discussion—management. Having Process KPIs visible for everyone to see in gemba is great, but at the end of the day, the question remains—what are you doing with the information? KPI displays can quickly become wallpaper if the data being displayed isn't effectively used to manage the processes. And who's the facilitator for this management? This should be part of the GL's responsibility. As we'll discuss in the next chapter, top management must support the GLs by allowing them time to manage both the tactical and the strategic initiatives in their areas. Although still somewhat reactive, the Process KPI management is also strategic from the viewpoint that new problem solving activities can and should be initiated when KPI targets are not met. The GL can also use the KPI displays to recognize trends before critical problems occur. This style of management is called "Gap Management," and this is the basic method used by Toyota to visualize where process improvements are needed (see figure 10.2 for an example of Gap Management).

Figure 10.2   **Example of (KPI) Chart Used to**
                       Visualize Gap Management

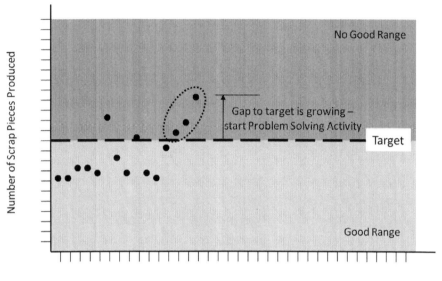

Remember, all Process KPIs are measurements of process conditions that include targets based on business objectives. These targets are aligned by drilling down company goals from the business plan or hoshin. The KPIs are then updated regularly by actually measuring various inputs and outputs of the process. The SFM system requires that this information is displayed for everyone to see and analyze. Finally, the variance between the target and the actual condition is managed by initiating problem solving activity whenever the desired results are not being achieved.

Notice that nowhere have I said that the goal is to "improve the KPI." Please keep in mind that the KPI is used to measure the capability of the process. At the point when problem solving begins, the focus should be on the process condition itself. The improvement in metrics should follow automatically when process improvements are made through good problem solving, i.e., the root cause of the problem is identified and countermeasured effectively. All too often, I've heard managers discussing problems with their employees by stating that the KPIs not achieving target must be improved. In my opinion, this is poor communication as a leader because the problem itself is misrepresented. What the team needs to understand is that the KPI underachievement is a consequence of a problem within their process. The process itself is what must be improved, not the KPI.

This is a very significant ideology and bears some further explanation. Applying TPS through effective SFM requires focus on processes not results. Subtle nuances in how management communicates with their employees can quickly shift the focus from processes to results. Processes can be difficult to improve because doing so requires the discipline of practicing good problem solving while applying TPS tools. Results, on the other hand, can be manipulated easily to reflect an immediate positive trend, and this is exactly what will happen if your team believes that you are simply managing numbers. Employees will soon realize that good numbers equate to satisfied management and praise, and they will manipulate numbers to reflect good performance even if the processes aren't effective.

Change Point Management (CPM)

The third and final element of SFM is change point management (CPM). A change point refers to any condition that triggers change in a process. The change could be small or large, planned or unplanned. The definition of what qualifies as a change point is really up to you. The key element of CPM is actually not the change point, it's the management. Managing infers that some deliberate action is being taken. In the context of CPM, this action involves reducing or completely eliminating the risk associated with changing conditions that might adversely affect the output of a process.

So what are some examples of change points? Anytime a new employee comes into an organization, a significant change point occurs. New employees bring many exciting opportunities, but they also bring significant risk—risk due to lack of training and knowledge, to inexperience, and to not being assimilated into the company culture. Whenever a new employee is first placed on the job there should be some form of risk management or CPM in place to safeguard both the employee and the company from possible mistakes and errors. Notice that I say "both the employee and the company." The employee is also at substantial risk when he is new to a job, especially if there are significant hazards associated with his work (as there are in most automotive processes). As a leader, you will need to decide what level of management is suitable for the risk associated with each change point. Keep in mind both the perspective of the company and the employee when you are assessing these risks.

Other examples of change points include modifications to process inputs such as new equipment, tooling, materials or work standards. New product launches would certainly also qualify in most companies as a significant change point. These are examples of major changes that would more than likely be planned. But what about a small change that is not planned? What about something as simple as a person being relieved from his process for a few minutes to take a restroom break? Would this qualify as a change point? I guess it would depend on how critical the process is and how skilled the person is who fills in for him during those few minutes. The point is, defining what qualifies as a change point can be very intricate and somewhat difficult. There are thousands of different scenarios that could impact your employees' work every day. Knowing what those scenarios are and gaining some clear understanding of their significance as a change point is the first step in establishing a good CPM system.

Once everyone understands what qualifies as a change point, it's time to start thinking about management. The first step is to make certain that everyone affected by the change understands the circumstances and the associated risks. What has changed? When did it change and for how long? What are we doing about the change to mitigate the risk? There is no CPM without effective two-way communication. Don't assume that employees understand what is changing around them and how those changes are being handled. Take the few minutes required to bring everyone into the loop and communicate what is happening. This is the first step of managing risk, and you will find that taking a few moments to get this step right may save you many headaches in the future.

Toyota has taken the communication of change points a step further by using communication boards to help visualize changes to their team members. At the beginning of a work shift or during the shift when significant, unplanned changes occur, team members would gather around the change point management board and review the information with their group leader. The board consisted of an area layout identifying the change point location, a log sheet where the details would be recorded, and other pieces of information relevant to how it was being managed. In this way, all change points could be tracked and communicated efficiently and also visually. This method was also particularly effective because multiple shifts of employees could review the same information at different times during the day. Passing change point details between shifts could create a "domino effect" when communication is not consistent and accurate.

The second and final management step in CPM is the action—what is being done to control the risk. All too often, I have observed perfect examples of change point communication and tracking, but the actual activity to manage it was completely ineffective. What do I mean? It's obvious to me that when significant risk is introduced into a process, some additional resources should be brought in to supplement and protect against abnormality. If for instance a piece of equipment breaks down in a process, it's not enough to simply back up the piece of equipment. There also needs to be some confirmation of the quality and the safety of the backup process. This confirmation doesn't have to continue indefinitely, but there should be some initial check to protect against substandard output. In TPS, the emphasis is on standardized work and processes, so whenever there is a deviation additional validation of results is required. Also, good communication and management of a change point isn't a license to violate TPS principles. All backup and supplemental processes used to manage a change point should be set up based on the same TPS standards as a "regular" process.

The most extreme form of managing a change point is simply stopping the process altogether. When the risk of abnormality is just too great, then stop what you're doing and get the process back into a standard condition. Doing this takes a lot of discipline. According to textbook TPS, when a process cannot be completed using the established standards, progress should be stopped until the abnormal condition is corrected (this is jidoka in the purest sense). Because this is often not practical and the risks can be effectively managed, a good system for CPM should be adopted and implemented as a safeguard against process changes. In this way, CPM is not contradictory to TPS principles because when managed properly a new standard is established prior to resuming operations.

My final advice for effective shop floor management isn't unique to Toyota, but the concept fits perfectly with Toyota Way thinking. To manage an operation successfully, you must be present and approachable by the organization. When I consider this style of management, I think of servant leadership—a phrase coined by Robert Greenleaf in 1970 when he published the book *The Servant as Leader*. My own reflection on servant leadership is simple—the positions in the organization subordinate to my own may be lesser in rank, but my position is secondary in importance. My existence in the organization is solely based on improving the work conditions for my team. I myself am successful when my team can perform their work free from disruption and with all the resources required to perform productively. How often do we get this ideology switched around and begin to believe that our employees are here to make us successful? Sure, there are people out there who have become successful riding on the backs of their employees, but this management style is not consistent with the Toyota Way.

Do you recall the following key points—effective TPS leaders go to gemba? The Toyota Way culture values contributions of all employees? TPS grew out of the Toyota Way culture (not the other way around)? Toyota was managing using the concept of servant leadership long before Mr. Greenleaf coined this phrase. It was out of necessity that Toyota management developed this style because the company was born out of virtually nothing. It was all hands on deck back in the early days, and this teamwork and supporting culture became the soul of Toyota.

Of course, there is a hierarchy of organization structure within every company—a reporting structure if you will, and Toyota is no different. Everyone has a boss and must answer to that boss. But that's not what servant leadership is about. I'm suggesting that as leaders, the mission is to put the success of the team ahead of their own. And if you happen to be a person who is driven by success, then you're in luck. When you focus your energy and efforts on making your team successful, in the end you will achieve all the best possible results.

In summary, consider the following points for successful SFM: Know your core business. Value the people who see to it that this core work is performed professionally and productively each day. Spend time in gemba, understanding the true current condition. Emphasize the importance of good processes developed using the best possible application of TPS principles. Listen to your employees and give them ownership of their work by sharing information with them regarding their process's performance. Effective shop floor management is how Toyota ensures that both TPS and the Toyota Way are being managed consistently everywhere that they produce vehicles.

CHAPTER 11
WHY STRONG FRONTLINE MANAGEMENT IS ESSENTIAL

As I've already said many times throughout this text, successfully managing using TPS requires a great deal of skill, discipline, and commitment. This statement holds true for every level within your organization; however, it's particularly significant for the frontline supervisor. Several different names are used in reference to this position—business leader, team leader, group leader, supervisor, area manager, and the list goes on. Job title aside, when I speak of the frontline supervisor I mean the first level of management, the primary level of exempt employee, and/ or the layer of management that is closest to your core business. Within Toyota, this person is referred to as the group leader (abbreviated GL). So for simplicity, I will use GL to identify the frontline supervisor.

I must tell you that over my career in manufacturing I've developed the highest appreciation for the people who perform the role of the GL. Not only is the frontline supervisor one of the most crucial operational positions in almost every company, but it's also one of the most difficult and stressful jobs to perform. The GL spends the majority of his time working in the heart of your company's core business, and as such, it's impossible for him to not feel high pressure and demands. For these reasons, senior-level management should have the utmost respect for people in these roles. The company as a whole can't be successful if these folks aren't successful. Later in this chapter, I will discuss the temptation to exclude lower levels in your organization from the TPS deployment activities. After all, everyone understands that the most important level in the organization is at the top—right? While it's true that commitment from the very top of the organization is necessary to successfully implement a Lean transformation, that's just the beginning. Ultimately, the role of senior management is to support the lower levels of the organization—not the other way around.

Let's begin this chapter by understanding the hard skills for deploying TPS and the role of the GL within that environment. Your business will certainly already have some established criteria for the roles and responsibilities of a GL, but please keep in mind that I don't know what those are. For me, I must go back to the model that I am most familiar with, and that all begins with the 4As. I'm going to assume that your GLs already have the ability to perform the work they are being asked to do, they understand their authority, their alignment to business objectives is clear, and there's some process in place for acknowledging accomplishments (and for accountability and consequences in the case of poor performers). What I hope to clarify in the next few pages is what the ability element of the 4As would look like for a high performing GL who is using TPS philosophies to perform his role.

Foremost in the category of ability is the GL's skill to recognize problems within his area of responsibility. Because TPS consists of tools designed to make problems apparent, you're going to want people close to the process who understand what those problems are. To do so it is my strong belief that the GL must be proficient in the standards of the work being performed by his team. Put differently, the GL should know the standardized work for every job that he supervises. How well should he know it? You'll need to judge this for your own individual business and operations, but my suggestion is that he knows as much as possible. Perhaps he cannot perform the work at the same pace (or takt) as the regular process operators, but at a minimum, the GL should be familiar with all of the elements and key points of work. The GL should also be knowledgeable of any equipment and raw materials used in his processes and be fully familiar with the overall layout of his management area. Perhaps all of this goes without saying, but for a GL to be able to assess an abnormal condition brought to the surface by TPS, he first must understand the normal operating conditions of his processes.

GLs can only acquire this necessary level of skill and knowledge when they have time to manage their area. All too often the frontline folks find themselves right in the middle of the mix—hands on, elbow deep in a process. Sure this can be a sign of high commitment and dedication, after all, the GL is jumping in to help out—right? Well, maybe. The problem is that when he's in the process making things happen, who's managing and observing how the processes are performing? In a non-TPS environment, perhaps the main emphasis or priority is on the achievement of results (you know, making the production number), but in a true TPS culture, the process itself is just as important as the results. For example, let's say that there is a piece of equipment not functioning in a process and the GL jumps in to back it up. For a short time, I would support this direction. By jumping into the process, the GL is (hopefully) allowing the operator to resume following his standardized work. If, however, this went on for an extended period of time, I would not approve of the GL backing up the equipment. The bigger picture problem here is, "Why is the equipment down?" not, "What are we going to do to keep the process running?" You see, the result of making the production number at some point should be balanced with the ability to smoothly run the process. This is a core discipline that must be developed when using TPS principles to manage—placing equal emphasis on both the short-term and the long-term results.

In this example, who should be leading the activity to correct the equipment issue—a maintenance person? Sure, maintenance is probably the right group to get the equipment repaired, but the work being performed in the process is still the responsibility of the GL. The GL's role isn't to just manage people in his work area, but instead he's the business owner of the entire process which includes each of the elements of man, method, machine, and material. When a GL needs support from outside functions (say, from maintenance in this case), he should ask for that support, but the ultimate responsibility for the entire process must belong to the GL. The concept of "full ownership" which I call self-concluding management is discussed in more detail in chapter 15. For our purposes now, let's just say that the GL cannot solve problems when he's working in a process or when lacking full ownership of the processes. Therefore, the GL must clearly understand these expectations and be provided with the resources necessary to manage his area successfully. The latter part of this statement is the responsibility of senior management and their commitment to the GL when TPS strategies are deployed.

Perhaps you thought that by deploying "lean" in your business, fewer frontline supervisors would be required? It's possible, but that actually depends more on how efficiently you are using these resources today than on your future staffing once TPS has been deployed. What I can tell you with confidence is this—your GLs will need to be able to recognize and solve problems in their respective areas, and they cannot do this if they are the backup operators or the vacation replacements. The GLs are going to need time (and other resources) to manage effectively using TPS as their business framework. Lean does not mean "running without" but instead should mean "running without waste." Having sufficient frontline supervisor resources to manage your core business is not wasteful. On the contrary—it's one of the best investments that your company can make to ensure TPS is followed successfully.

In chapter 9, we discussed the importance of process measurement. As the complete process owner for his area, the GL is the facilitator for managing the Process KPIs. An effective GL will utilize Process KPIs to make the conditions for his processes visual for the employees working in the area and for upper management alike. The GL can then lead continuous improvement activities by prioritizing any conditions that are not achieving targeted performance levels. By displaying the KPIs, the GL can communicate with and engage his employees on a daily basis. Please keep in mind, however, that the GLs are going to need time to pull off this level of shop floor management. One of the biggest complaints from my GLs at Toyota was that there just wasn't enough time in the day for them to do all the required management tasks. Think about it this way, the GL is the closest person in management to your core business and the direction of the business is to operate using Lean/TPS principles—right? Then doesn't it stand to reason that the most logical people to manage your Lean operations are the GLs? Wouldn't providing them with the resources to effectively manage be in everyone's best interest? Of course, it would be, and even Toyota struggles sometimes to make this happen.

So the GL is operationally the "business owner" for his processes, but what is his role strategically—say in the area of process improvement? Multiple times throughout this book I have referred to TPS as being an organizational strategy, meaning that everyone, from the entry level to the highest level of management, is responsible for understanding and practicing the principles of TPS. There's no way around this point—TPS philosophies must be imbedded in the culture of the company. It doesn't really matter how well the executive team understands and believes in TPS if the grassroots level of the organization cannot apply the principles effectively and believe that this is the right way to manage. As such, the GL must be well trained and knowledgeable in the application of TPS. In order to be the "business owner" of the daily operations, wouldn't it also make sense for the GL to take control of his own destiny by also owning the process improvement efforts in his area? Well, this is exactly the approach that Toyota takes, but I see other companies failing in the area of kaizen because their approach is vastly different. This just happens to be another one of those areas where I feel many companies are completely missing the mark when they attempt to copy what Toyota has done with TPS.

What I'm seeing outside of Toyota is a heavy reliance on "Lean teams" to deploy TPS and advance continuous improvement initiatives. Even if this approach has yielded some success for your business, this is NOT (and I say emphatically—NOT) how TPS was meant to be managed. Presumably, these teams have been specially trained in TPS theory and application, and as such, they become the "experts" for TPS in the organization. This is another concept that is not shared within Toyota. There are no TPS experts. There are only varying levels of expertise and experience in applying TPS in the workplace. The teams are then deployed throughout the operations and various projects and kaizen activities are undertaken. But my questions are: Where is the GL when these Lean teams are coming into his area to fix problems? Do they have any buy-in to the activity? What role does the GL play in the kaizen activity? What role does the GL play after the kaizen is completed? From what I've seen in my limited exposure to companies using this approach, the GLs aren't involved much, if at all, when kaizens are being made in their areas.

Here are my issues with using this method. First, most of the time the TPS or Lean/Six Sigma training takes place in a classroom with some "laboratory" applications. At best, this approach will give your people a theoretical understanding of TPS principles, but can they apply their learning practically in the workplace? After all, this is where the action is, not in some classroom, and this is precisely where the GL spends all of his time—in gemba! Second, the idea of creating a Lean team of "experts" is nonsense in a true Toyota culture, and after all, isn't this the culture you're trying to emulate? TPS knowledge is passed slowly from teacher to student through a process of experiential learning. There are no shortcuts. TPS is learned hands on, in the trenches, out in gemba. How much actual process experience does the Lean team have? Do they have more practical experience than your frontline supervisors? Finally, the use of Lean teams to deploy TPS in the workplace is not sustainable. Let's face it, when outsiders come into a work area and "help" by bringing new ideas and operating methods without having practical experience, how well would you expect this to be received by the GL? Is it possible for the GL to build equity in improvements made without his support? When the Lean team leaves to move on to the next problem area, the GL will be stuck holding the operational responsibility. If kaizens don't support the GL's needs, he won't waste time sustaining them.

This is precisely why Toyota deploys TPS from the floor up. The core business starts at the floor in each process, so in order to sustain TPS thinking and principles, the people performing the work must understand TPS. But how can you practically teach everyone in your organization TPS principles and application? You can't, at least not with the snap of your fingers as some companies would like. You will need strong frontline supervision that can not only manage the daily operations but can also train and develop their team. Within the Toyota culture, the Group Leader is the primary resource used in training and developing employees. This includes both the process training needed to carry out the core business (the standardized work if you will), and the TPS skills and knowledge that all employees will need so they can continuously improve their processes. The employees are going to improve their processes? That's right. The true intent and the power of the kaizen we spoke about in chapter 2 starts at the process—or improvements made by the employees working in gemba. Sure, an organization can appear to be implementing some kaizen when they have Lean teams blitzing the operation to improve efficiencies here and there, but these results cannot be sustained over time. Sustainment only occurs when TPS is understood and practiced at the grassroots level of your organization.

I know this must sound like a broken record and also sound somewhat arrogant to many readers, and for that I apologize. This explanation isn't meant to question your ability to manage your business. What I do want, however, is to save you time and resources in going down a path that simply will not work. Why do you think Toyota has always opened their doors to outsiders? Does it seem strange that Toyota would offer public tours of their facilities to everyone—even to direct competitors? They do not feel threatened by other companies' ability to copy what they are doing. Heck, anyone can pick up a book and read about

TPS and the Toyota Way, but there aren't many companies out there that have actually taken this information and achieved what Toyota has. In studying the TPS practices of other businesses, I've not found a single company that is trying to deploy TPS at the grassroots level. That doesn't mean that there aren't some companies out there doing this, but predominantly, the approach I'm seeing is the Lean team/top–down approach.

OK, so you don't want to copy Toyota's operations exactly. You want to make your own strategy, one that uses elements of TPS but also incorporates other tools such as Six Sigma or some of Deming's teachings. That's fine, but I will advise you that if you take this piecemeal approach toward Lean deployment, you are not going to accomplish the results that Toyota has achieved and sustained for over five decades. That's not how it works. It's an "all-or-nothing" system. Again, there is no easy way, no shortcut, and no compromises. You cannot implement TPS using a top–down strategy and leave the process employees on the sidelines. If you have done this in the past and struggled, take a minute and question why this hasn't been effective. TPS works because it is a bottom–up system. It is designed to work at the core of your business—where the real work is happening. This is why you must have strong management on your front lines. Your GLs are the key to implementing Lean, not your senior management team or a Lean team.

Now that I've beaten this point to death, let's move on to another thought—have you ever asked yourself how your employees see your company? When "Joe Employee" thinks about his employer, with whom does he associate? When a friend or a family member asks him how he likes his job, who in your company influences his opinion? You? The CEO or the COO? The plant manager or the president of your facility? Chances are that unless you have a very small business, most of your employees rarely, if ever, associate themselves with senior or top management. For better or for worse, most workers see their company through the actions and behaviors of their direct supervisor. Are you familiar with the phrase, "A supervisor is the face of the company?" If not, think about this for a minute. Your employees view the decisions that your frontline supervisors make as a reflection of the company. When you have strong supervisors who support your employees and help them grow and develop, your employees will have a favorable opinion of your company's respect for people and for the company overall. If, on the other hand, your GLs treat your employees with indifference and have no interest in their personal growth and development, your employees will translate this into an uncaring company. It makes good business sense to provide support personnel who can assist the GL with functional roles such as training curriculum development and planning, but at the end of the day, the GL must take an interest in developing each employee and recognize his role as the "face of the company."

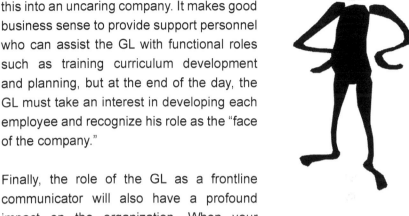

Finally, the role of the GL as a frontline communicator will also have a profound impact on the organization. When your company is operating normally, there isn't much time for anything else. A routine day consists of your employees coming to work, performing their job, taking a couple of breaks and a lunch, and then going home. In an eight-hour day, Toyota builds dedicated time into the work schedule for GLs to communicate with their employees. The lines are shut down. There is no other agenda. The purpose for this time is to ensure that all employees have some knowledge about what is happening in their company—after all, it is their company too. The ability of the GL to communicate effectively is paramount. The information comes from the GL's mouth, but the interpretation comes from the dozens of people hearing the words. Clear, relevant information builds employee trust and confidence in the company. Poorly communicated gibberish breaks down trust and leads to misinformed employees who lack job commitment. This isn't a good formula when you're trying to build a disciplined team capable of working productively using TPS. Good, two-way communication is the glue that will hold your highly capable workforce together, and you'll need highly capable, confident GLs to make this happen.

Certainly every position in your organization is significant or it wouldn't exist. No one can afford to do business with employees at any level who provide no support for the bottom line. That being said, I really want to stress in closing this chapter that the GL is probably the most overlooked and underestimated resource utilized by Toyota. There are many little nuggets of information in this book that provide insight as to why Toyota has been able to achieve and sustain a high level of operational effectiveness using TPS principles. None of these nuggets are more significant than understanding how and why Toyota has developed strong frontline management. Group leaders mean everything to Toyota's success. They are the tacticians, the floor managers, the process improvement leaders, the lead trainers for their employees, and, ultimately, the face of the company. I'm not sure why so many businesses are trying to deploy Lean strategies while leaving the GLs on the sideline. Perhaps it's just easier to train a "so-called" group of TPS experts and bring them to the floor while the GLs maintain operations. This may seem like a good strategy, but in the long run, there is just no substitute for developing and retaining strong supervisors. Having strong, capable, and confident frontline supervisors has always been a key ingredient to Toyota's success.

CHAPTER 12

EMPLOYEE DEVELOPMENT

Had I chosen to arrange this book based on the level of importance of the subject matter, I could have easily made this one of the first chapters. But why is employee development so important? Both applying TPS and solving problems will require a highly skilled and continuously developing workforce. The days of achieving results through brute force effort are a thing of the past. Today's workforce must be smart—there's just no two ways about it, and the best companies will make employee development part of their core values. In this chapter, I will discuss some of my personal philosophies regarding development, and I will also briefly describe two of the techniques used by Toyota to ensure that TPS and problem solving are practiced skillfully.

At the foundation of my human development philosophy is the concept that all people can and should be developed to improve their capability. As a leader, you should also share this belief. Anything less would be an admission that an employee has no potential for acquiring more skills and knowledge. And who has the right to decide if another human being can grow beyond his current capability? Presumably, good leaders will not limit their organization or any individual. They should constantly challenge their organization to stretch beyond their current capabilities, and they should bring everyone along for the ride.

I also firmly believe that people instinctively want to grow and learn. God made people differently than the rest of his creation. God created humans in his own image to be caretakers for his earthly kingdom. As such, it stands to reason that God himself wants people to be smart, to have deep understanding, and to have the capacity to grow intellectually. How else would we be prepared to look after this earth and all of its resources? But clearly not everyone appears to be growing and developing. Just look around and you will see people who seem to lack motivation and appear to be slumbering around, doing nothing but taking up space. So how do these people fit into my development philosophy of "people instinctively want to grow and learn"?

It's been my experience that a person who appears to have lost the initiative to grow and learn is usually the one who has been labeled (either through words or actions) as someone who cannot improve. Ask yourself this question—who usually gets the best development opportunities, the person who has the biggest development needs or the person who is already the most capable? Typically, it's the latter person, and in my opinion, the reason is because there's no effort or preparation required when opportunities are given to currently capable people. This is the short-term, easy decision to make. Development is difficult because it requires intentional effort. As a result, those who develop quickly and require the least amount of direction are appealing to supervisors (and to teachers). This is another classic case of "taking the path of least resistance." The result is that capable people who can develop ability more quickly continue to be attractive candidates for future opportunities while those people who require more time to develop skills become labeled as lazy, unteachable, or low performers. But in this scenario, who is really lazy and lacks initiative—the low performer or the person who avoids the opportunities to develop him?

Before I get too far into my development philosophy, I'd like to share a diagram that I've created to help visualize the concepts I will discuss further in the first half of this chapter (refer to figure 12.1). Although the terminology used in figure 12.1 is quite common and familiar, I would like to first define several of these terms in the context of how I would like for you to understand my philosophy. (I realize these aren't necessarily the accepted dictionary definitions, but please don't let this distract you from the message of the model.)

Figure 12.1

A Model to Visualize
My Human Development Philosophy

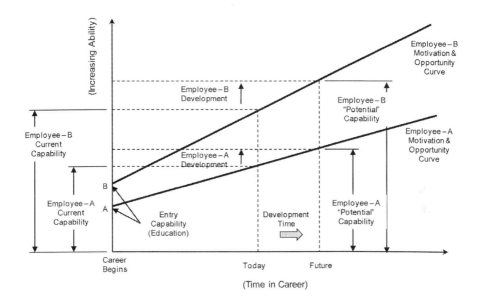

(Time in Career)

Definition of Key Terms:

1) Ability—A combination of acquired skill and knowledge.
2) Capability—Any individual's current range of ability.
3) Development—Intentional activity targeted to improve ability and thus expand a person's capability.
4) Potential—A reference to someone's capability at some time in the future.
5) Motivation—A person's drive to improve his own ability and thus expand his own capability.
6) Opportunity—Management providing the necessary resources for employees to develop.

So what exactly is happening in this diagram? My intention in creating it was to clarify how I interpret a person's development over the course of his career. In order to visualize this, I have created a simple X/Y coordinate system with the vertical axis measuring "Ability" and the horizontal axis representing "Time in Career." Intuitively, most people will agree that over the course of a career, an employee's ability will improve or increase. The two bold lines on the field of the chart represent the potential of two employees, Employee-A and Employee-B, over the time spanning their careers, and both of these lines support the notion that ability improves over time. The difference in the slope for the two lines is based on the differing Motivation and Opportunity for each person. I'll explain momentarily the significance of this difference, but for now, just recognize that these two bold lines represent two uniquely developing employees.

When looking at the point where both lines intersect the Y-axis (at the point where their "Career Begins"), you will notice that Employee-B begins his career with higher capability than Employee-A. Why might this happen? Perhaps there was a difference in formal training and education or maybe there is a difference in work history prior to beginning their careers with your company. Regardless of the reason, for the purposes of explaining this model, let's just agree with the premise that new employees can begin their careers having different levels of capability.

Now look further to the right on the X-axis at the point labeled "Today." When tracing upward from this point to the location where a vertical line intersects the "Potential" lines for the two employees, the corresponding "Current" level of capability can be seen to the left on the Y-axis. From the time each employee's career began until "Today," the gap between the capability of Employee-A and B has grown, but why? Of course, the original gap was attributed to difference in entry level capability, but after spending an equivalent period of time in their respective careers, Employee-B is pulling away in ability. Of course, in the model, this occurs because the slope of the two employee "Potential" lines is different (again, the steeper line belonging to Employee-B), but in the "real world," I believe this occurs because of one of the following conditions:

1) Employee-B has higher motivation to acquire new ability.
2) Employee-B has been given more opportunity to develop ability.
3) Employee-B has both a higher motivation and has had more opportunity to improve ability.

Because one or more of these three conditions will determine the future potential for both of these employees, I would like to discuss why I believe these conditions exist in a little more detail.

Starting with motivation, what factors can you think of that might influence someone's motivation to grow and develop? I certainly believe that some individuals have a personal drive that they have developed over time—perhaps because they had parents who encouraged them or because they have been rewarded for past development achievements. Some people also discover personal motivation from participating in sports where they are driven by the desire to win, to be successful, and to achieve an ultimate goal. Whatever the reason, motivation that moves a person into action must initiate within the person himself. (At least, I've found this to be true of adults who hold the fate of their own destiny. Young children, on the other hand, can be motivated into action by others.) There's an old Buddhist proverb I really love that goes something like this—when the student is ready, the teacher will appear. This is exactly what I mean when I say that everyone must have some personal motivation and take initiative for his own development. A teacher cannot help someone improve unless he first wants to improve. Yes, teachers can "appear" before the unmotivated, but the development won't take root because the soil for growth isn't ready.

A related development saying that resounds with me is—No person can learn if he already knows everything. Yes, believe it or not, none of us are all-knowing, and we never will be. The motivation to learn comes from that place deep down inside where a person humbly realizes that he doesn't know everything. And humility can be a great motivator for development. After all, who needs development when they're already perfect? My favorite place to find examples of people who find humility to develop is in the sports community. Consider how much time the world's best athletes spend working with trainers, coaches, and other teammates to improve their ability. At the professional level, an athlete's skill is already considerably differentiated from the "Average Joe," but those with the highest personal motivation desire to stand out from even the best in their profession. The Michael Jordans of this world humbly seek out others who can help them find those few skills that they have yet to master. I believe this motivation is slightly different than the drive to win and be the best. Many of these individuals have already succeeded at the highest levels of their profession. No, this kind of high self-motivation comes from recognizing that even when you're the "best," you still have more potential.

How can an organization motivate an individual to want to develop? One possible method for engaging employees in their own development is by rewarding them for investing in their growth. Since development is mutually beneficial for both the company and the employee, why not give some special recognition to the employees who are making development a priority—an honors list for employees so to speak? Positive recognition is a very powerful motivator, and what better way to show that your company cares about development than by making a special effort to bring attention to those who exemplify the company's values. How many employees are going to want to step up once they associate acknowledgement (remember the positive "accountability" of the 4As?) with personal growth? I'm not talking about monetary rewards. I'm talking about including a special article in the monthly newsletter about an employee who has achieved a personal development milestone. I'm thinking more along the lines of holding a simple reception after work for employees and their families when they have gone beyond expectations for development. Simple, positive recognition supporting personal growth efforts will send the right message to your organization—development is valued by this company.

Notice that I didn't say that development is a "high priority." The difference is this—priorities change, but values generally stay the same. When a company values development, it is committed to providing the necessary resources for every employee to improve his ability. This is a great segue into the second condition—providing opportunities for development. Providing opportunities for development is the responsibility of the company and of the supervisors who are managing the careers of their employees. But who generally gets those opportunities—every employee equally or only the best and brightest? Asking yourself this question is a great litmus test for determining if your company values development or if it's only a priority for a few select people. Before I get too carried away with this thought, let's consider the idea that the overall population of your workforce represents a "normal distribution" of talent and ability. Figure 12.2 will help us consider this point more thoroughly.

Figure 12.2   <u>**What is a Normal Distribution?**</u>

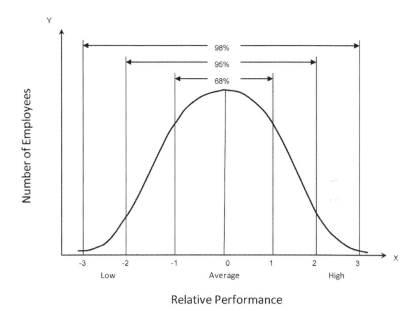

Relative Performance

The normal distribution shown in this figure represents the classic "bell-shaped curve" that you probably recall from your academic days. (Do you remember celebrating when the professor adjusted the test scores based on a "bell curve"?) Normal distributions are considered to be the most prominent statistical probability model and they are used throughout the physical and social sciences as a simple illustration of complex phenomena—say to understand the distribution of relative ability inside your organization. Within the population of any workforce, there is a distribution of ability that when measured (however you typically measure performance) and displayed, it looks similar to the normal distribution shown in figure 12.2. The area under the curve represents the population of people having various levels of ability—from "Low" to "High." As you might expect, the number of employees performing at the extremes of both "Low" and "High" ratings is relatively small. Compared with other companies, I'm sure the relative number of "exceptional employees" in your organization is impressive. However, this distribution is created by comparing the ability of the people only within your own organization. What I really want you to notice is that the majority of the population of your company is performing near average. Within a normal distribution, the area under the curve defined by plus or minus one standard deviation represents approximately 68% of the area—or in this case your workforce (a standard deviation refers to how far a point is from average. The area within six standard deviations of a normal distribution represents 98% of the sample population). Stated more simply, statistically 68% of your workforce performs either slightly below or slightly above what the company defines as "average ability" or performance.

This number is much higher than many people realize, and that's why I want to take a minute to consider who is getting the development opportunities in your organization. I've worked for companies where the best development opportunities were "reserved" for only the highest performers in the organization (statistically this represents only about 10–15% of the workforce). This group typifies the third condition mentioned previously in my development model—highly motivated employees who also benefit from exposure to many development opportunities. But why would these individuals require preferential opportunities for development? My theory is that the top 10% of your performers are similar to those exceptional professional athletes I was discussing previously. The top performers are probably in this category not because of anything that you've done, but instead because of what they've done for themselves. High performers have acquired their ability because of their self-motivation. Yes, having exposure to opportunity has certainly helped, but most of these people would have found the opportunities on their own. That's what makes them the top performers.

What you should be asking yourself is how can your company continue to achieve increasingly more aggressive performance targets when 68% of the workforce performs with near average ability? Can your employees learn and utilize a highly disciplined management system like TPS, given the fact that most of them have near average capability? If you are skeptical that this model fits your organization, ask your HR team to plot out the bonuses paid to your employees over the past couple of years. If your company practices a "pay-for-performance" strategy, then this analysis should paint a fair image of the organization's distribution of talent and performance. I'm betting that what you'll find is a normal distribution with the majority of your employees gathered near the center of a bell-shaped curve.

Here's my point—the high potential employees don't need as much help as they generally get. They're where they are because they are truly exceptional—even without preferential opportunities and support. The group that really needs your attention, however, is the team in the middle of the pack—the average ability group. Without a doubt this group represents the lion's share of your workforce population. By sheer numbers alone, this should warrant some concern from your company's leadership. My philosophy is pretty darn simple—make employee development a value, and spend the majority of the company's resources developing the majority of the employees, not just the few at the top.

Now here's the final point I'd like to make regarding my development model—the "Motivation and Opportunity" curve for each of your employees can change. The slope of this line isn't really fixed even though the original model shown in figure 12.1 would seem to imply this. What would happen if you as a supervisor took some special interest in your section and began intensifying the development efforts for all of your employees—even for the average folks like Employee-A in my model? With additional opportunities and improved motivation, is it possible that the potential for Employee-A might increase (as shown in the revised diagram in figure 12.3)?

Figure 12.3   <u>**Improving Employee-A's Potential**</u>
<u>**Through Intervention**</u>

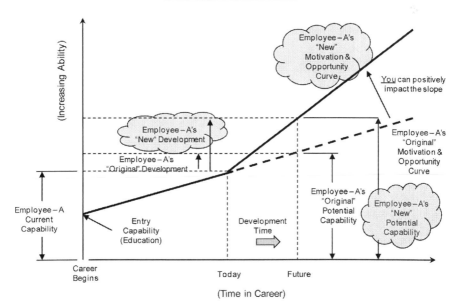

I realize that this is merely a visualization of a simple model, but think about this concept for a minute. Can you impact someone else's potential by taking more interest in his development? Is a person's future capability already determined, or can it be improved with targeted development? By encouraging employees and making development a company value, you *can* positively impact the motivation of your workforce to improve their ability. And by making targeted development opportunities available to all employees, you can increase the "average" capability of the entire organization. Improving the overall knowledge base of the organization is how good companies become great companies.

Notice that up until now I haven't used the word *training*. Training is a tricky word, and I will only use it sparingly. Actually, I have quite a hang up with this word, especially with human resource people who think that the key to human development is "more training." Truthfully, my attitude toward human resource groups in general gets pretty twisted because what I've encountered is that they typically place more emphasis on managing staffing numbers and policies than on managing the careers of their employees. But I digress . . . I do agree that some types of training can be beneficial when the purpose is targeted and the information taught in the training can be put to use immediately. All too often, however, the training does not fit these criteria. How many times have you gone to training because it's the standard for the company—you know, the training that comes in multiple phases that everyone must complete? And then once you get your "ticket punched" by completing the training, do you ever apply what you learned to your work? If the training wasn't targeted for your individual needs in a specific growth area and for a specified purpose, chances are you will never develop from what you've been taught.

Training that seeps into your brain and goes no further is simply "information." It will get filed in your memory bank for a while along with everything else that you've heard or experienced. Maybe you'll remember it later and maybe you won't—at this point it's just "information." If, on the other hand, this newly acquired information moves you and stirs up some passion, then what you've learned has "inspired" you. "Inspiration" is deeper than simply data storage in your memory bank. "Inspiration" is stimulating and pushing you to respond to what you've learned. It's the spark that may lead you to actually doing something.

When you leave a training session where you've been inspired and you actually use the information that you've learned, this becomes "application." The desired outcome of development is this final stage, and when reached the efforts of both the teacher and the student come to fruition. However, my experience has been that the final stage of "application" is rarely achieved after most training has concluded. This is why I'm not a big fan of "training," and why in this chapter, I will be discussing alternative methods for employee development (methods other than typical classroom training that is).

There are two common development processes used within Toyota that I'd like to highlight for your consideration: (i) OJD—on the job development, and (ii) *jishuken*. OJD isn't a new learning approach, but the Toyota spin may be a little different than what is practiced traditionally. OJD within Toyota begins with a supervisor and a direct report collaborating on a targeted, specific dimension of development. The performance dimension is not relevant to this discussion, but what is significant is that both parties acknowledge the development need. How often have you disagreed with your supervisor on your development areas—say after an annual performance review? This is another factor supporting the concept that "the student must be ready before the teacher will appear." If you've been forced into a development "opportunity" and you have no personal buy-in, the chances of successful growth are pretty slim.

Another key element of OJD is that the development process itself is connected to work which supports existing business initiatives. The goal is to link current work plans when assigning skill development projects to avoid creating "busy work" or special activity aimed solely at development. Like most companies, Toyota is strapped for the resources required to carry out their core business, so taking on new projects for the exclusive purpose of development would be wasteful (or at the very least an additional burden). Utilizing existing business initiatives for training purposes basically kills two birds with one stone. The work is going to be completed anyhow, so why not also take advantage of an opportunity to improve an employee's skill and knowledge at the same time?

Taking advantage of existing business commitments for development purposes does create some risk for management and for supervisors. After all, who would normally be given the assignments when pressing forward with existing business objectives—an unproven, underdeveloped employee or someone who already has the proven capability? Chances are that the latter occurs more often than not, but giving every challenging assignment to an expert does not create the needed environment for learning. As I stated previously in this chapter, giving assignments to those with existing capability epitomizes management taking the path of least resistance. At best, this is a short-sighted approach with focus mainly on achieving immediate results. Continuing down this path will limit the growth opportunities for the business. I see this style of management from people who lack vision or are inspired only by achievement of results. Usually, these folks are trying to make a name for themselves and racking up some quick, favorable results is the best way to do this. On the other hand, choosing the path of development is a longer-term approach that focuses on increasing the overall skill and capability of the organization for the future. This strategy tends to shift priority from an individual (say from the supervisor's career aspirations) to the longer-term success of the team.

How does Toyota manage the risk of developing employees while simultaneously pressing forward with established business plans? Well, as you might have guessed, the "safety net" in this strategy is the supervisor (or the person leading the OJD project). The OJD leader becomes both a teacher and a secondary resource to ensure that the business objectives of the project are being met. Once the development need is identified, the assignment is made, and the objectives are clearly communicated, the leader will schedule a series of periodic progress reviews with the "trainee." During the reviews, the trainee will share findings and developments directly with the leader and/or the supervisor—preferably in gemba. These review sessions serve two purposes—coaching for the employee to ensure that the development areas are being thoroughly explored, and progress reviews for the supervisor to make certain that the business priorities are being met.

The preferred coaching style to encourage learning on the part of the employee is sometimes described as "Sherpa coaching." The term *Sherpa* refers to the guide used for mountaineering expeditions in the Himalayan mountains, particularly Mount Everest. The role of the Sherpa is to recognize conditions that will be dangerous to the climber and then suggest possible solutions. The Sherpa does not make the decision for the climber, but instead serves as an expert source of information and possibility. This is the ideal approach for the OJD coaching as well. Solutions are not given, but rather the leader will use his own personal experiences and knowledge to provide alternatives and/or options whenever the student reaches milestones and decision points in the project. The goal is to proceed with the business objectives while maximizing the learning opportunities. In the end, the employee has learned by doing—by experiencing the previously unfamiliar development dimension firsthand. The supervisor has invested in the overall ability acquisition of the organization—making it stronger and more prepared for the future.

The second development technique used frequently within Toyota is called jishuken (pronounced "jish-ew-ken" and loosely translated as "self-study"). Now, there are many different practices of jishuken within Toyota which in my opinion is a direct result of the method used to pass knowledge from person to person within the company (i.e., everyone learns the history and the practices of the company from a slightly different perspective). One common interpretation of jishuken is "kaizen blitz" or PKA (practical kaizen activity). Certainly, jishuken activities will involve some improvements or process kaizen, but my understanding of jishuken is slightly different than this. I will be discussing the method of jishuken that I was first taught at TMMI because this is the most pure application of jishuken, and it's the practice with which I am most familiar.

Usually, organized kaizen activities are initiated solely for the purpose of improving an existing, known problem area. In contrast, a jishuken activity is targeted at developing TPS skill and application. So when a typical PKA activity is conducted, the ideal participants are those who already have highly developed TPS skill, whereas jishuken activities are generally performed for employees requiring some TPS skill improvement. Theoretically, a jishuken could be conducted anywhere within the operation, but similar to the OJD thinking, the activity is commonly carried out in an area already identified with a specific business need. So although the primary focus will be on developing TPS skill and application, the jishuken itself should also drive some improvement to daily operations.

The leader of the jishuken is always someone who has deep TPS knowledge and skill. Many times during my career the jishuken leader was the most senior-level TMC employee in the department or maybe even in the plant (our Japanese president led jishuken activities when I was a manager at the TMMI facility). The jishuken leader serves as the facilitator, the coach, the motivator, the judge, and many other roles. The most significant characteristic of the jishuken leader, however, is that he be a "seasoned veteran." The leader must be someone that the jishuken participants recognize and respect as an expert in both TPS principles and in the practical application of TPS in the workplace. Someone who only has "book smarts" in TPS will not be respected by the participants because they lack experience in the "trenches." In this sense, I would consider jishuken to be a very "blue-collar" hands-on activity, and therefore, the leader must be someone who's willing to roll up his sleeves and jump into the fray.

Occasionally, jishuken activities have a set ending point, and in other cases, the jishuken will continue until the leader determines that the activity is complete. In either case, the participants receive personal coaching with hands-on application of TPS principles. There is no classroom—only gemba. When thinking about how Toyota develops people, I immediately associate with this jishuken style of learning—intimate coaching in a small group or even one-on-one, engagement at the process in gemba, and practical application (experiential learning). It would not be uncommon for an employee at Toyota to participate in several jishuken activities each year. My analogy for good jishuken is this: jishuken is to a Toyota employee as the gym is to an athlete—neither gets paid for working out, but the workout helps develop the stamina and the skill required for their core job.

The best characteristic about both OJD and jishuken is that this style of development is facilitated internally—Toyota's managers and supervisors training Toyota's next generation of leaders. What better way to show employees that a company values development than to take personal initiative and invest of one's self? This is why I say that the development "potential" or the slope of the line shown in figure 12.3 can be changed when a supervisor takes personal interest in his employee's development—I've seen it myself! And I can tell you firsthand that there's nothing more satisfying than seeing someone turn around his performance because of time that you as a supervisor have committed to helping him. Sure, you can save some time and even make yourself look good by focusing on strategies to achieve results today, but I just don't know how any business can survive long term using this approach.

Here are a few last thoughts on development. Value and respect the ability of your people. I once had a boss who referred to my career potential only in terms of what the company could provide for me. What he failed to acknowledge is that I own my capability—not anyone else. And all of your employees are the same way. You have no proprietary rights to the skill and knowledge that your employees have acquired. They own it, and they will take it with them wherever they go. My advice is that you respect the knowledge and tap into it as often as you can. Allow employees to showcase their expertise by training others. Reward development by acknowledging those who make personal growth a priority. Retain your company's storeroom of knowledge and treat it as though it's one of your most prized assets. After all, the development of your employees is only mutually beneficial if they stay with your company.

Finally, as a leader at any level, one must always believe that his employees have the capability to grow and develop. Granted, some people have a higher aptitude than others in this area, but everyone can learn new skills and advance the quality of their work. Once you stop believing this, you've given up on your employees. Someone who you believe has no potential for growth is dying in the organization. Don't give up on your employees. Have confidence in their ability to learn and inspire them to grow personally. If you've got an employee that just doesn't belong in your organization, then you owe it to that person and to the rest of your team to let him go. If, on the other hand, an employee is worth retaining, then he's also worth training. Make development a value, not a priority. Your ability to successfully apply TPS management in your organization will depend on the knowledge and skill you develop.

CHAPTER 13

EMPLOYEE ENGAGEMENT EQUALS SUCCESS

By now, my concept of employee engagement in a TPS culture should be of no surprise to you. In almost every chapter of this book, I have tried to emphasize the bottom–up, employee-driven methodology required to make TPS both successful and sustainable. TPS isn't a blitz activity conducted by a few experts; it's a way of business, a mentality, a set of values by which your business operates. Sustaining a TPS culture requires effort and deliberate activities centered on engaging your employees.

The most basic engagement method for employees stems from the 4As management approach discussed at length in chapter 6. To summarize, your team will stay engaged when you provide them with the necessary resources and allow them to perform their work autonomously. In short, you must give them ownership of their job. Let your employees be creative and perform their work within the scope you've defined in the authority of the 4As. Nothing will engage your employees more than satisfying their need to "own" part of your business, to make daily contributions, and to see success through their individual accomplishments.

Allowing employees to improve their own work by giving them authority for process kaizen is another great way to ensure their engagement. When team members can freely suggest improvements for their processes, they will work more productively with higher commitment, and overall, the company will see great benefit. After all, that's what employee engagement is all about—realizing the collective benefit from commitment to a common purpose. And kaizen is how employees improve their work conditions, benefiting themselves as well as the company. The employee is the primary beneficiary of process kaizen because he realizes the immediate impact of the improved work conditions. The company is the secondary recipient of the kaizen benefit, due to some extent because the workforce is more committed and fulfilled. I don't know how to measure this benefit to the company, but I can tell you that it does exist. Back in chapter 6 in figure 6.2, I introduced my concept of "Understanding Why You Are Succeeding," the relationship between employee engagement and management capability. I must admit that I haven't confirmed the social or behavioral science behind this correlation, it's just my theory. But my theory is based on over twenty years of observing human behavior in a factory, and what I've discovered is that highly committed employees can overcome many adversities. By providing a culture where commitment grows, your company will benefit because employees are willing to do almost anything to ensure success.

But practically speaking, when will employees have time to improve their processes? How can you keep people interested in kaizen when they're spending the majority of their time performing their job? Creating time for kaizen requires investment on the part of the company. Because employees cannot practically improve their processes while they're working, they will need to be given time outside of normal business hours—time specifically earmarked for kaizen. Toyota calls time dedicated to kaizen "quality circle" time—a reference carried over from TMC when employees were given time to work specifically on quality improvement ideas. Eventually the term *quality circle* became a more generic label for all types of process improvements, not just quality. The amount of time given will depend on the amount of investment that your company is willing to make. Some of the kaizens will have definite, tangible payback that can be realized in cost savings or future cost avoidance. For these kaizens, the justification is simple to calculate in terms of cost versus benefit. Not all kaizens will be financially this straightforward, however, so it's important that you always consider the less tangible benefits from improving employee engagement as well as the tangible financial benefits.

On the flip side, one sure way to ruin your employee engagement is to reduce TPS to nothing more than a process used to lower cost by eliminating headcount. Consider this perspective—why would any employee want to help you find waste in his process if it could lead to him losing his job? No matter how dedicated your employees are, this just doesn't pass the sanity test in my book. I know that many companies do implement TPS and Lean strategies solely for the purpose of eliminating "extra" processes. These tend to be the same companies that utilize "Lean teams" as well because no employee in his right mind is going to help eliminate his own job. The irony is that I'd be willing to bet that in almost every situation where Lean teams are being used to reduce headcount, the resulting reductions don't last for more than two or three months.

Here's why I'd be willing to make this bet. All people and/or processes exist for a reason (remember my theory of organizational equilibrium?). Think about it—people don't just walk in the door of your company and start working, do they? Somebody put them there, and unless you understand what's going on behind the scenes prior to eliminating a process, people are going to eventually return out of necessity. You see, the "extra" person in your workforce isn't the "real" waste in the process. The extra person has been placed in the process to accommodate whatever the real wasteful condition is. This underlying, hidden wasteful condition is what must be eliminated and then the need for the extra headcount will also disappear. Identification of the real waste is why you need the help of your employees because they understand what is really happening in their process.

Cost can and should be controlled by eliminating unnecessary work, but not at the expense of losing employee engagement and commitment. This is how Toyota has managed for over fifty years. No Toyota employee has ever lost his job as a result of a kaizen. The solution requires a balanced approach and good communication. First, let's discuss the approach. If your business normally experiences fluctuations in demand, consider adding some flexibility to your staffing by incorporating a percentage of short-term contract employees along with your fulltime staff. These workers can be brought in under the condition that their work is temporary which won't create any false expectations for future employment. As business conditions change (either from demand fluctuations or due to processes reduced through kaizen efforts), you can retain integrity by releasing only those employees whose short-term contract has expired. The downside to the short-term employment commitment on the company's part is that you're also going to receive a short-term emotional commitment from the temporary employee. Don't expect the same level of emotional commitment that you would see from one of your fulltime folks. This just isn't realistic—the cost of improved flexibility is lower employee commitment. Believe me when I say that this cost is worth the benefit you'll gain from building trust from your fulltime employees that kaizens will not be used to eliminate their jobs.

Every business also has normal attrition. No matter how much a company is admired by their employees, some people will inevitably leave for one reason or another. Understanding the normal rate of attrition is also important when planning efficiency improvements. Let's imagine that your business's normal annual attrition rate for the fulltime workforce is around 5%. If you were able to improve efficiency by this same rate, normal attrition would accommodate the planned headcount reduction. The reductions can be accomplished by transitioning employees from processes eliminated through efficiency improvements into areas where attrition has left holes in the organization. Of course, the timing of these moves will almost never align perfectly, so this is where the strategy of creating a "kaizen team" makes perfect sense (and this is how and why Toyota uses their kaizen teams).

As processes are eliminated due to normal efficiency improvements, use this situation to develop some of your employees by giving them an opportunity away from their normal job—i.e., in a kaizen team. To accomplish this, move the person from the job that was eliminated through kaizen efforts and train him in the process where the employee needing a development opportunity works. This employee can then be moved to the kaizen team where he can learn and practice new TPS skills. When using this strategy, management not only makes an investment in an employee's development, but also the entire organization benefits when the kaizen team finds other waste opportunities elsewhere in the company. Wouldn't this be a wise investment versus simply taking the eliminated employee and letting him go? You see, eliminating reduced manpower immediately is a short-term approach that will never yield any more savings than the original headcount reduction itself. The approach of investing human resources in kaizen teams is a long-term investment, and like any investment, the sky is the limit on how much return the company might possibly realize.

The long-term method is preferable to me because it's a win/win strategy. The company is investing in additional cost savings and efficiency improvements, and the employees are being rewarded and benefit from the development they are receiving as a kaizen leader. Instead of destroying employee engagement by focusing solely on headcount reductions, you could actually improve employee engagement and commitment and still become more efficient. It really all depends on your approach and your intentions. Are you in it for the short term, or are you in it for the long term? Do you want to parlay your team's commitment into even greater profitability for your company or are you content with the dollar you saved today? In the employees' eyes, the approach you take will reveal much about your true intentions for their future and for the future of the company. Short-term decisions will translate into, "They don't care about us, and we have no future here," versus long-term decisions which will translate into, "I trust this management team because I can see them investing in our future." Ask yourself which team you would rather have working for you.

Job security alone won't motivate and commit your employees, but it will bring some peace of mind to most rationally thinking people. As with other areas of a successful TPS deployment, communication will be key to building trust when choosing a long-term efficiency improvement approach. You'll need this trust factor for sure, a benefit you should already be realizing from the relationships you've built by spending time with your people in gemba (chapter 10) and from developing highly skilled frontline supervisors (chapter 11). Open and honest, two-way communication regarding how the company's manpower efficiency will be managed is a healthy way to build trust, maintain high employee engagement, and ensure that process kaizens address the real issues that usually only the employees themselves truly understand (i.e., the root cause of the problems versus symptoms).

Can you see how all of these strategies come together? I just don't know how to implement one without the other. Deploying TPS really does require a holistic approach. Strictly applying the TPS "textbook" thinking usually doesn't work in the practical world. That's precisely why I've written this alternate "textbook"—to explain a practical approach for deploying TPS that is capable of achieving the efficiency benefits that most businesses desire while maintaining balance with the "human side" required to sustain the results.

I must admit that because of my engineering background, I rarely read the instructions for anything. I can generally figure out how to assemble the grill or use the new tool without resorting to instructions. And if I didn't know any better, I'd be tempted to deploy TPS without reading an "instruction manual" as well. It doesn't seem that complicated. Most of the concepts are pretty straightforward. You don't have to be a rocket scientist to understand the idea that eliminating waste is good for your business. How hard could it really be? Well, even Toyota who has dedicated most of their company's history to deploying TPS struggles and makes mistakes. Even Toyota has team members who lose engagement and fall short of the "ideal employee" we imagine.

I just hate to think about how many companies have been sold a bill of goods by "peddlers" of Lean who really don't understand (or at least don't teach) these finer points of TPS deployment. I know that the desire to reduce cost is very real and there's a thirst for wanting to know the secrets of TPS. But I also know that there's a lot of poorly executed TPS going on out there because I've seen the aftermath. I envision a group of people blitzing through a facility while employees are left trying to understand what is happening. I imagine little to no employee involvement and lots of fancy talk, charts, graphs, and presentations. I see short-term results that are not sustained over time. Mostly, however, I see an organization that is left picking up the pieces while trying to figure out why TPS doesn't work. What went wrong?

Employee engagement is another one of those Toyota "secrets" to sustaining TPS. I really want to see other companies have more success with this, but first you've got to believe that it's not as simple as being able to memorize the tools of the TPS house. This is why I say that textbook TPS and practical TPS are two completely different things. The textbook application can be attempted by anyone while the latter relies on holistic management and leadership capable of seeing beyond the savings that can be achieved today.

CHAPTER 14

THE VALUE OF FUNCTIONAL EXPERTS

Does your company have a career path for every employee? Many of the best companies do, and in my opinion, this is one of their defining qualities. Great companies recognize the value of their employees' talents, and as such, they plan for their future. We've all heard the saying that "employees are a company's most valuable resource," but what does this really mean from a practical sense? How do you ensure that all of your employees recognize not only their current value to the company but also their future potential for growth within the company—a career path if you will?

Over the course of my career, my viewpoint on the topic of career paths has evolved from seeing absolutely no value in them to believing that they may be one of the single most important elements of job satisfaction for many employees—especially newer employees. From the beginning of my career, I knew that I wanted to be the leader for whatever team I was on, so for me, the promotion from engineer to supervisor and finally into senior management fit perfectly within my career goals. However, my own "fast-track" career path into management was probably the single biggest contributing factor to my early ambivalent attitude toward career paths. I only knew one direction—that of promotion along the management path of the organization. It wasn't until I actually started supervising professional employees that I began to consider alternate views. For example, was it possible that someone could actually find enjoyment and fulfillment in his career by staying in a functional, support position? I began to wonder what types of opportunities existed for someone content to be great at performing a professional skill versus a managerial skill.

The professional skill and knowledge that I am referring to is something that I call functional expertise. But functional expertise isn't only the skill and knowledge attained by having a formal education for a specific occupation. It is much more profound than this. It is the "deep smarts" that is acquired over a career of performing professional work within a specific role or field. Functional expertise is developed experientially and therefore takes time to attain. You can't just go to school and become an expert (even when you stay in school and earn an advanced degree). Textbook experience is good if you're planning to become a professor or do research in a laboratory, but if you plan to work in the business world, then you're going to need some practical experience to supplement the book smarts.

In your own organization, think about who those "go-to" people are when the toughest problems must be solved—those are your functional experts. Are these people the heads of the departments or are they found in the middle layer of the organization? From my own experience, I have learned that experts can be found almost anywhere. However, the further one progresses along the management career path, the tendency is to broaden overall knowledge and sacrifice some functional expertise. As such, the best bet is to look in the middle of the rank and file of the organization for your functional experts.

The "function" of functional expertise can be technical as with the example of the engineer, or the role could be more administrative such as the role of human resources, purchasing, or cost accounting. Very few organizations are made up of a single function or profession, and as a leader, it is important that you recognize what those functional roles are within your company. While I was a manufacturing manager at Toyota, I often overlooked the other vital functions required to support the manufacturing operations. As much as I might hate to admit it, manufacturing wouldn't have survived without the support roles that ensured that no detail of the business was overlooked. The point is that most organizations are going to have many functions housed under the umbrella of one company, and although the professional roles for each of these functions may be vastly different, they are equally important to the success of the business.

So what difference does it make? As long as your company has a viable process for evaluating employee performance and ensuring that the best performers continue to rise to the top, isn't that what really matters? What I have come to realize is that this is not necessarily the case. The shortcoming is that all too often the "decision makers" of the company will judge an employee's growth potential based solely on his performance and motivation to advance in the company. The employees who are earmarked as "high pots" (or high potential for future growth opportunities) are generally those who have both great performance and a strong desire to be promoted. Is there a process to recognize those who are great achievers although they're motivated to perform as functional experts? Are initiative, drive, and ambition only associated with those motivated by promotional advancements into management?

This chapter is my call for you to question this aspect of your company's culture. Can your employees feel valued and rewarded when they are content to perform well in their current role? After all, everyone cannot be the next department manager. Just look at your organization structure. Surely, there is a pyramid shape with fewer and fewer advancement opportunities at the most senior levels? Logically then everyone is not going to be able to advance, but does that make them less valuable to the company? If you have employees who perform well below expectations or they have a poor motivational fit with the company, then you many need to consider some corrective action. This discussion isn't about dealing with poor performers. On the contrary—I want you to think about how you inspire your good performers to want to continue down a path of success within your company. If employees can only associate their success with opportunities to be promoted, how many of your employees will be left feeling like a failure?

If some of these questions make you stop and think for a moment, then there's a good chance that your company has a "one-size-fits-all" approach to career paths. The problem is that management or supervision isn't for everyone, and as a leader, it's your responsibility to understand where employees will perform their best work and find the most satisfaction in their career. Some of the most brilliant engineers that I ever met were some of the worst managers that I ever worked with. What happened to them? Did they get promoted and stop trying? How did they go from being some of the best functional experts to some of the lousiest managers? I personally don't believe that these guys stopped trying or performing. Instead, I believe that their careers were being managed by people who didn't understand their personal goals and strengths.

The "one-size-fits-all" career path tends to have this effect because the assumption is that all high performers must want to be promoted. In this case, someone should have understood what these engineers wanted, where they found fulfillment in their work, and how they could be motivated in ways other than a promotion into supervision.

In the course of my own leadership development, I have certainly come to appreciate the value of rewarding good performance. This is after all a very powerful motivator. So how can functional experts be motivated and rewarded when they are content to stay in a non-managerial role? I would suggest starting with career paths that encourage professionals to develop functional expertise. Some of the best practices that I've seen in this area come from companies where "senior" ranks are withheld for employees with the highest proficiency in their chosen profession. Growth into these ranks is similar in significance and with pay advancements similar to a promotion, although the position itself does not involve supervision. Supervision is a separate career path from the professional career path. In this way, the "senior professional" is rewarded financially while also being recognized for his achievements and expertise in his chosen professional area. Having dual career or advancement paths for professional and managerial promotion will provide incentives to a broader range of employees and help those of you who are currently suffering from the "one-size-fits-all" method.

The benefit of valuing functional expertise for employees is pretty straightforward, but what about the value brought to your business? From my perspective, the benefit to the company is in having employees performing in their "sweet spot," the area where they perform the best because they enjoy what they are doing and they're very good at it. Most if not all of us could spend our entire careers working on improving our weakest performance areas, but the fact is that we benefit more from leveraging our strength areas—the areas where we perform the best and find the most fulfillment with our work. Don't believe me? Take a close look at your last ten annual performance appraisals, and see if the areas where you need development aren't the same every year. What about your strongest performing areas? I'll bet they're the same too, but why do these patterns exist? They exist because you generally leverage your performance strengths and they continue to develop while your weaknesses tend to stay the same over time. Nobody will ever be perfectly rounded. The development effort required to level up a "weakness" is significantly higher than the effort required to further improve on a "strength."

If an employee has some "derailer" type behavior or performance issue (you know, the type of problem that has him standing with one foot already outside the door), then this qualifies as more than just a "weakness"—it's a potential career ender! You're going to have to deal with these extreme performance issues regardless of career paths. What I have come to realize, however, is that many of these "derailer" type issues and behaviors develop initially because people are placed into roles that are bad career fits—say an engineer who has become a supervisor. Given the opportunity to advance professionally, many of these poor job fits can be avoided and the resulting "derailer" performance issues might just become a thing of the past.

Another benefit to the company is that functional experts can make great coaches. If you're looking to grow your organization from within, what better way to do it than to have experts for every professional role in the company? This is precisely how Toyota has passed their skill and knowledge from generation to generation over the past fifty years. Remember the OJD training method discussed in chapter 12? These functional experts are the people Toyota uses to lead the OJD development activities. And for many employees, there is no greater sense of accomplishment and recognition than to be utilized as a trainer and coach. Notice that I didn't say "all" employees. Not all of your professionals will be good trainers, and they will not look at this as a reward or an opportunity. Remember that we all have different strengths and weaknesses. Some people will be better teachers than others. For those who do enjoy teaching others, recognition of their expertise in this way will provide extreme motivation and job satisfaction.

And what happens to employee retention when there are more career path opportunities in your company? I believe you'll find that more employees will feel better job satisfaction, and as a result, the company will retain more professional skills and knowledge. This must be good—right? As with successful sports teams, I have always believed that the most successful businesses attract and retain the best people. Are there exceptions to this? Probably, but it only seems logical to me that if you want to be the best at something, then the resources for accomplishing that "something" should be the very best that you can afford. Placing value on protecting resources is something that I learned from my grandfather. He was the type of guy who never owned anything unless it was the best available. He wasn't wealthy, but he would save his money until he could afford to get the best value for his dollar—performance, quality, durability. His opinion (which he obviously passed on to me) was that the best work is produced by the best tools (or resources). Once he owned the tool, he ensured that it lasted forever. It was after all an investment.

The truth is that people really are a company's most valuable resource, and your functional experts are one of the best assets in your organization. What good is the "tool" if you don't take care of it? In the case of an employee, what value does the company retain if the person leaves? Keeping employees motivated by creating career growth opportunities is essential to retention, and your people want to understand their potential. Your best employees should know that they're the best, and the future plans for their careers should also be well known to them. Skilled people who aren't retained are lost resources to a business. Think of it this way—if someone stole a laptop from your business, would that be upsetting? Wouldn't you take every action necessary to ensure that the assets of the company are protected? Well, that laptop has no value other than the replacement value. It has no capacity to work or create on its own. The person that you might possibly lose however has endless value—or should I say potential? Which is more worthy of your protection efforts?

Many of your finest employees would be completely satisfied to work professionally in their chosen field if they were assured of some level of reward, recognition, and career advancement. When promotion into management ranks is the only career path, employees will choose advancement over job fit, and both the employee and the company will suffer. Everyone has a strength area where they perform at their very best, and management or supervision may not be that strength area for everyone. That's why we work as a team—to complement each other's strengths. When we recognize that people really are the most valuable asset of the company, perhaps we will structure our human resource management to reflect this. Today, companies are spending millions of dollars safeguarding their electronic information against theft, but they are investing very few resources to ensure that their employees feel secure with their career path, their future. Does this make sense?

The final take-away? When your company commits to a Lean transformation as I'm describing in this book, you will invest thousands of hours training, practicing, and implementing the TPS tools. You will also spend countless hours engaging your employees as you create the company culture required to nurture and sustain a Lean management system. While you *might* be able to reload your organization with Lean skill, rebuilding and realigning your culture is a very difficult thing to do when your workforce turns over due to attrition. To maintain your Lean culture, you're going to need to retain your people. Valuing functional experts is one way to do this because you will be giving your employees more options for their career growth. It's also a great way to ensure that people are aligned in their best performance area—another plus when using a sophisticated management system like TPS.

CHAPTER 15

SELF-CONCLUDING MANAGEMENT

In the last chapter, I described how valuing functional expertise can motivate some employees who have no desire to advance along the management and supervision path of your company. In this chapter, I will explain a much different approach used to develop and encourage people who do want to pursue a career in management and supervision—self-concluding management or SCM. I was introduced to this concept by the first president of TMMI, Mr. Seizo Okamoto (a very beloved man who was known to his employees simply as Mr. O). I believe Mr. O formed the SCM concept at least partially out of necessity to support business conditions created by Toyota's rapid expansion from Japan into practically every corner of the globe. So before introducing the components of SCM, I should briefly explain the history of Toyota's speedy growth over the past few decades.

Many times already I have mentioned that one-on-one experiential development and training methods have always been used by Toyota to teach TPS and Toyota Way skills. Of course when applied within a single facility or manufacturing site, pulling together the resources required for this style of intimate development is relatively simple. But can this same method be applied when new operations are spreading thousands of miles away from where the training resources reside in Japan? Well, this scenario is exactly what Toyota has faced dozens of times over the past twenty years or so. How were they able to sustain worldwide growth while staying true to the company's philosophy of passing down skill and knowledge experientially?

Toyota's global expansion of manufacturing facilities burdened TMC's senior management to consider many different economic and business variables.

However, no decision was more significant than choosing which existing TMC site would fulfill the role of "mother plant" for the new transplant. (New facilities outside of Japan are often referred to as "transplants" or "child plants.") The role of the mother plant is actually just as you would imagine—caring for and nurturing the employees in the new location until they were "mature" and had developed sufficient capability to function on their own. In this role, as with actual parenthood, the mother plant never completely leaves the child plant, but instead, they are always available to guide and support them in any way needed. For the TMC plants, being chosen to be a mother plant was a great honor, and the role was taken very seriously. After all, the mother plant was responsible for creating the foundation for the child plant's manufacturing capability and for their corporate culture. Essentially, the efforts of the mother plant would determine the future path for either successful or failed operations for the child plant, and the failure of a new facility was never an option.

So practically speaking, what is the role of a mother plant, and what does this role look like in application? First, the mother plant was expected to supply people as resources to support all organizational levels and functions within the child plant—from administration to manufacturing, from senior managers to trainers who worked directly in gemba with the production team members. During the first several years of a transplant's operations, the president of the new facility was also always a senior leader transferred from Japan (thus Mr. Okamoto's selection to be the first president at TMMI). Why was this so important to TMC?—For the same reason that TMC wanted to support the new facilities with a mother plant. Both strategies ensured that regardless of how far away the child plant was physically located from Japan, the culture would most assuredly be Toyota-Way-based and managed using TPS philosophies.

Up to the point that Toyota began to expand globally, very few TMC personnel had been used to train anywhere outside of Japan, so the skill and knowledge of Toyota was for the most part retained within Toyota City. With new operations starting all over the globe, TMC was faced with the challenge of transferring their TPS capability and their Toyota Way culture outside of their home base. This was a huge hurdle for the mother plants because the majority of their employees spoke only Japanese, and their training materials were also not translated into any other languages. Although there were many training resources already available to help teach new employees the tools of TPS, the

Toyota Way was not documented until well after the initial global expansion had begun. To learn the Toyota Way, new employees would need to experience the Toyota culture through working at existing Toyota facilities and by training side by side with experienced TMC managers and trainers. This meant that TMC would be required to dispatch Japanese employees all over the world while also creating training opportunities for the new transplant employees at their own facilities inside Japan.

Back in the late 1990s when the TMMI plant was being built, Toyota was simultaneously growing in other parts of the world. The rate of Toyota's growth was unprecedented, and the capability of TMC to dispatch their most qualified and experienced people was a strain to their local, Japanese operations. The production at the Japanese plants was at full capacity in order to accommodate the record automotive sales during this part of the decade. But as important as meeting this sales demand was to Toyota, they were willing to make the investment to send their most capable resources to the new overseas plants to ensure they were trained properly. You see, Toyota didn't let the urgency of the current market conditions overshadow their value for conducting business the Toyota Way.

This is where Mr. O's image of SCM originated. Realizing that Toyota's rapid expansion was placing a significant strain on TMC's resources, Mr. O would challenge his new management team at TMMI to deploy SCM—a strategy intended to create self-reliance from TMC resources quickly and effectively. In other words, Mr. O wanted his management team to develop TPS application skills and a Toyota Way thinking methodology in the shortest time possible. (Perhaps you too might find this concept of value?) This in turn would minimize the development burden of resources from the Japanese plants (in this case the mother plant for TMMI was the Tahara Plant in TMC).

Mr. O's vision was simple. To quickly develop his new managers, the TMMI organization would be structured flatly with very few layers of management. This arrangement would facilitate independent thinking, quicker decision-making, and more ownership of individual department resources. There would be no finger-pointing at the "other guy" when things didn't get done because there was no other guy! The effectiveness of the managers would depend on their broad capability in a variety of dimensions: technical (mainly vehicle assembly processes and equipment), administrative (creating and managing budgets, business plans, staffing, and training), and the ability to lead a new organization. The only requirement for deploying this strategy was that these "single layer" management positions would need to be filled by individuals who already possessed broad capability for manufacturing. Fortunately for Mr. O, his vision became a reality because in 1996–97, the desire to work for Toyota was high, and they were able to take their pick of capable managers from various other manufacturers throughout North America.

I was fortunate enough to be one of those early additions to TMMI's staff when I was hired as an assistant manager in late 1997. Having come from Ford, I was familiar with vehicle assembly operations (the technical side of building cars that is), but TMMI's organization was nothing like what I had experienced in the past. In my initial role at TMMI, I was responsible for production and maintenance operations in the assembly area. I also took on a significant role in staffing and policy creation for assembly and for the entire facility. This broad scope and responsibility was consistent with SCM. I was hiring the people and writing the policies for the area which I would later manage once mass production began. Essentially, I was paving the path of my own destiny. There were no barriers preventing me or any of the management team from creating the business structure we needed to be successful. It was a high risk/high reward environment, and for me personally, I found this time to be the most rewarding of my automotive career. All that mattered was creating a successful team that could build the best pickup trucks in the world.

Each area had the same structure with one manager responsible for all functions in his section—production, maintenance, engineering, logistics, and pilot activities. There was collaboration from outside functions in the areas of safety, quality, cost management, and human resource management, but these resources were to be used solely as support. The primary role of the non-manufacturing functions was to establish processes and procedures at the company level. Of course, this was done to ensure consistency across each manager's area (more the "what's expected" part of the business), but the "how to do it" part was left up to the managers.

Each manager was also assigned a Japanese advisor, a seasoned senior manager from TMC with operational experience in a similar capacity at the Mother

Plant. The advisor's role was to do just this—give the manager advice on how to run the business the Toyota Way. Manufacturing based on the Toyota Way wasn't intuitive to the North American-trained management team, and especially the practice of gaining consensus among the Japanese and the American managers was initially a painful process to learn. Even though the organization was relatively flat with very few layers of management, the few that did exist were expected to gain consensus on virtually every decision made within the company.

Working so closely with a single advisor gave the manager quick insight into the Toyota Way of operations and decision-making. The personal working relationships formed between those first advisors and the managers were like a brotherhood that lasted well beyond those startup years. What we later came to realize was that Mr. Okamoto wasn't just building a management team and forming a company culture, he was also creating a family. Mr. O's SCM organizational structure was not only flat and lean, but it was also very intimate. Everyone on the management team, both American and Japanese, learned to rely on one another. Learning from each other became natural and enjoyable because we built a bond of trust before we ever built the first Tundra pickup truck.

So management did grow and develop quickly out of necessity. The startup of the TMMI plant was an extremely busy time, and every manager felt stretched to the very end of his capability. Often, these stretched roles put people in new situations, facing challenges well beyond what they had previously faced in manufacturing. As a personal example, while working at Ford, I had never hired or even interviewed any of my hourly employees. This was a function of human resources, not of manufacturing. When starting up TMMI, I must have interviewed and hired literally hundreds of people, many of whom are still working at that plant today. It was a responsibility that was new to me, but the skills and lessons I learned from this experience will last a lifetime. In the SCM culture, nobody ever waited for the next person to pick up the ball and run with it—at first because there was nobody else, but later because we embraced the challenge of getting out of our comfort zones and learning new management skills.

When company-wide problems arose or direction impacting the entire organization needed to be discussed, the small team of managers could be quickly assembled, and decisions could be made without a lot of fanfare and bureaucracy. In this way, the organization was nimble and effective, and because direction was set through gaining consensus, there was always enough diversity of thought to ensure that decisions were never pushed through due to any one person's agenda. Cross-functional development was occurring because the consensus process forced managers to hear and to understand each other's viewpoints and priorities. Building consensus really did make us a closer team, and our respect for others grew as we came to understand the different perspectives and personalities of our peers.

The flat organization also made teaching and confirming the new managers' TPS skills simpler for the senior Japanese advisors. Daily jishuken was the preferred method for developing the managers' capability. Many of the first jishuken activities were led by Mr. Okamoto himself. Dedicated time was spent daily for walking through the plant with Mr. O as he would challenge us to think more deeply about what we were seeing in the manufacturing processes. Our solutions were always contested and new approaches or methods would be suggested. Mr. O could do this because his management team was small. He could personally instruct and confirm the understanding of his entire management group, because this team was deliberately sized to accommodate close, personal contact and coaching. As a point of contrast for those who may not be familiar with automotive operations or manufacturing in general, the plant manager at the Ford plant where I formally worked was rarely if ever in gemba. The thought of him having any contact with me or teaching me anything personally was the furthest thing from my mind.

As with many of the other lessons learned during this startup period at TMMI, the jishuken activities and the personal learning opportunities led to extensive TPS and process knowledge. We were able to learn the practical application of TPS quickly and effectively because our training was hands-on, and it was happening in real time as we were running our daily operations. We could instantly see the results of what we had applied in our jishuken learning. Moreover, the visual nature of the activity and the personal involvement at all levels of management made it possible to efficiently pass knowledge and learning points throughout the organization. Our direct reports were learning from us almost simultaneously as we were learning from the senior Japanese staff. Are you familiar with the phrase "The best way to learn is to teach"? Well, this is exactly what we were doing. The classroom was the plant's manufacturing area, and the class time was every day while we were performing our normal roles within the plant.

So if SCM was so successful, why the almost 180-degree difference in philosophies between functional expertise at the middle levels of the organization and the broad responsibility approach of the self-concluding management at the higher levels of the organization? These two approaches may seem somewhat contradictory, and in many ways they are. But bear in mind that the roles at each level of the organization are completely different, and these two approaches were developed based on these differences. This is a great example of the concept of developing people with a purpose in mind which was discussed in chapter 12. Because the desired development outcome is different at various levels of the organization, there should be separate strategies deployed for each. One development method may not achieve the desired results for everyone.

For example, at the middle levels of the organization expertise in a certain function is very desirable. I want accountants who are the best at calculating rates of return on investments, process engineers who know machine design and equipment inside and out, and safety specialists who know everything there is to know about OSHA, National Electric Code (NEC), and all the National Fire Protection Association (NFPA) standards. There's a tremendous amount of detail in each one of these functional areas that as a manager I will need to tap into. I also want to reward the individuals who aspire to become professionals in these roles. This is why I place value in functional expertise. I want my professionals to feel capable of growing and contributing to the company for their entire career. Again, not everyone's career goal is to be the next plant president and see their potential from the perspective of being promoted into a supervisory position. There should be alternate growth and development paths for your professional employees.

In the top management levels, however, I want people who have well-rounded backgrounds—jacks of all trades but not necessarily an expert at any of them. To effectively supervise using the 4A methodology (a methodology that I developed years after Mr. O taught me self-concluding management), a manager cannot micromanage. He must rely on his subordinates to function in their defined role and direct and support them only as necessary—teaching and coaching rather than doing. There's nothing worse than having a boss who's the expert at what you're trying to do! Good luck pleasing that person, and oh by the way, if he's spending so much time interested in what you're doing, what else could he possibly be accomplishing? Managers should manage and leave the "doing" up to the experts. SCM effectively stretches a manager's roles creating an environment where "doing" just isn't feasible. I must admit that this approach can be very frustrating for some people—especially those who consider themselves "hands-on" managers. My thinking is that when an employee enters the ranks of supervision, he must begin to surrender parts of his functional expertise in lieu of fulfilling his management role—again teaching his skills rather than jumping in and performing the functional work.

Has your organization ever promoted someone from within the company to a supervisory role and then left him in the area where he once performed a functional role? If so, then perhaps you've witnessed firsthand why a supervisor must surrender some functional expertise in order to develop into an effective manager. In my career, I've seen where the practice of promoting within one functional group has led to subordinates who feel micromanaged functionally while being undermanaged in the areas of growth, development, communication, and creation of a shared vision and direction. In other words, their new boss who was formerly a peer continues to work in the same capacity, and therefore, the management of the group suffers. By flattening the organization and combining roles and responsibilities more broadly at the higher levels of management, supervisors will be less likely to step back into performing functional work.

Self-concluding management may not be the best strategy for every organization. Even within Toyota, the Indiana plant was the only facility that deployed this strategy, and only during the startup years when Mr. Okamoto was the president. After Mr. O left TMMI and new senior management stepped in, the structure of the organization changed. Layers were added and roles were aligned more functionally throughout the organization. One could argue that having more managers who have less individual responsibility will make operations more effective—after all can't more be accomplished when focusing on specific tasks? Perhaps, but there is also a greater risk of becoming complacent and lazy, and don't ignore the possibility of missed development opportunities because people have been silo'd into very narrow roles and scopes of responsibility.

However, if you feel that your organization needs some "leveling" to stretch out the roles of your management team, applying SCM principles could help you achieve higher levels of self-sufficiency, broaden development opportunities, and improve the speed of your team's decision-making. I thoroughly enjoyed the time I spent in an SCM organization because I was more challenged and I developed more management skills than at any other time during my career. The use of this strategy just might come in handy when beginning a Lean transformation because your top managers will be forced to rely on lower levels of the organization versus doing everything themselves. The grassroots, process level is after all where you'll want your Lean strategies to take root, so consider how your organization's structure can help facilitate this growth.

CHAPTER 16

PROCESS
SELF-COMPLETION

I have saved this topic for one of the final chapters because process self-completion (or PSC) was one of the last strategies that I helped to develop while employed by Toyota, and it incorporates many of the ideas I have already mentioned. In this chapter, I will also discuss several key reflection points from Toyota's failure to manage according to TPS and the Toyota Way. The concept of PSC came about due to an outbreak in quality concerns with various Toyota vehicles in 2008. Specifically, several significant corrosion issues escalated to the point that Toyota was forced to issue a recall, and the senior management within TMC became concerned that Toyota was losing their competitive edge for quality in the marketplace. Now it might be debatable among automotive experts (and even consumers) if Toyota still held a competitive quality advantage at this time, but the fact remains that Toyota internally was feeling the pressure of quality falling below expectations.

So what changed? That would be the million-dollar question, and nobody really knew what had changed. None of the issues reported in the field were associated with manufacturing defects within the Toyota plants themselves. The recalls were related to either product design concerns or parts supplier issues. In spite of this, Toyota began to reflect deeply on the speed at which they had grown over the previous decade. Was it possible that the expansion of Toyota globally had led to some sloppiness in the planning and execution of their design and manufacturing processes? Had the DNA of Toyota become weakened due to resource depletion? Many insiders felt that these concerns were valid, and it was decided that the heart of Toyota's culture and DNA was where improvements were to be made—immediately!

The first step was for all Toyota management to reaffirm that their core business and the area of their operational effectiveness was manufacturing. After all, expertise in manufacturing through application of TPS principles is what allowed Toyota to be successful in the past, and a "grassroots/back-to-the-basics" attitude began to emerge. Within TPS specifically, the focus was directed toward elements that could positively impact quality systems, and the logical place to start a grassroots activity was at the foundation of TPS—or the foundation of the TPS "House" if you will (see figure 16.1).

Figure 16.1   **The TPS "House"**

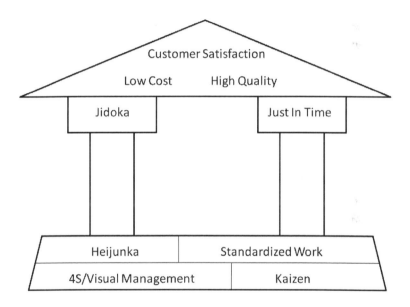

As discussed throughout this book, applying TPS requires a holistic approach. No element of TPS is intended to be utilized as a stand-alone system. In this case, however, the initial focus for quality improvement could be isolated to two main areas—standardized work and jidoka. TMC's concept was that if each team member performing the work could guarantee good quality from his process, quality will always be built into each vehicle from the ground up. Sounds simple right? Well, yes and no. In the past, there had always been significant emphasis on developing complete and detailed standardized work and training the team members to perform this work precisely. The process of jidoka, to not pass a defect on to the next process, was also deeply rooted in Toyota's manufacturing. But what TMC was questioning at the heart of this quality improvement initiative wasn't the "what" but the "how" of TPS. In other words, how did each team member know assuredly that the standardized work he performed on every vehicle was executed flawlessly before allowing that vehicle to move into the next process? Sure, everyone at Toyota understood that this was what was supposed to happen, but how was jidoka really being followed in gemba, and how did we, as management, know for sure that it was happening consistently?

The reality is that the average takt time (or production rate) of the assembly facilities is approximately 65–85 seconds which translates into team members having between a minute and a minute and a half to do their work, confirm it, and make a decision regarding the quality of what they have done. This cycle then repeats approximately 350 to 450 times per day for each team member. Because of this high frequency and the sheer number of processes required to produce a vehicle, no one could definitively state how each team member confirmed that every vehicle had been built properly in his process. What we did know is that the standardized work was complete and detailed, the team members were trained, critical processes were controlled and monitored, and all internal audits and inspections of the vehicles indicated that quality was within current standards. This is how each plant had been managed for years, but now the status quo was being questioned. Senior manufacturing and quality managers throughout Toyota were being directed by TMC to develop a method to *ensure* that each process was being performed to exacting standards. Moreover, the requirement was that each team member must have the capability to judge the quality of his work by himself while meeting production takt time. This corporate initiative became known as process self-completion.

What makes PSC so difficult to appreciate is that every automotive assembly facility has hundreds of unique processes (perhaps near one thousand in TMMK's case). Adding to the complexity of this task was the lack of standardization in approach from TMC. Yes, the desired result was well understood, but there was very little direction or standard methodology to achieve this desired result. As such, the local plant management teams were left to devise their own plans.

My discussion from this point forward will be based solely on the development and the execution of my paint and plastics departments' PSC strategy while I was at TMMK. Although I did initiate many of the concepts and the vision for this PSC approach, I cannot take sole credit for the process I am about to describe. Many other talented engineers and managers were also involved in developing this method.

The major steps in my PSC strategy can best be illustrated using a pyramid with execution of the steps progressing from the base to the peak of the pyramid (see figure 16.2 below).

Figure 16.2   **The Process Self-Completion Strategy**

One characteristic of this PSC strategy that should jump out immediately is that almost all of the elements found within the pyramid are already utilized to some extent within Toyota. I was convinced that we already had a robust process for quality control, so our focus should therefore be on finding improvements in what we were already doing. We were, after all, still a world-class manufacturing organization, and there was no need to reinvent the wheel. Clearly, the quality problems Toyota was experiencing were real, and they could not be ignored. I knew there were still holes in our systems, and to find them, we were going to have to start back at the very beginning of our quality processes. We couldn't make any assumptions about what we were doing, and there were no existing processes or systems that would be off limits to our scrutiny.

PSC was also the first strategy where I incorporated the 4A approach to deployment of a new management system. Yes, I had used the 4As several times to level up individual processes such as the waste segregation example discussed in chapter 6, but PSC was on a much grander scale than anything I had attempted up to this point. The 4A philosophy was still not followed at TMMK outside of my areas which added to the uniqueness of our PSC strategy. Despite these challenges, I still thoroughly believed that using the 4A approach was necessary to build integrity with our team members and to get my organization managing at the grassroots levels of TPS and the Toyota Way. By 2008, I had spent nearly two years with my leadership team discussing the importance of managing successful performance using the 4A approach, and I was confident in their capability to apply these concepts consistently throughout my organization.

The PSC strategy begins at the base of the pyramid shown in figure 16.2 with the "ABILITY" block. Contained in this block are the elements Standardized Work, PFMEA, and Professional Skill Development. As a recap from chapter 6, the emphasis of the ABILITY is on improving the skill and knowledge of the team members performing the work. Before we could focus on any other improvement factors, I wanted to ensure that we had provided all of the necessary conditions for a good process to the team members so they in turn could perform their work successfully.

Standardized work should not require any special explanation, and for the most part, there were no significant changes to it in our PSC strategy (at least not until we reached the much later step of PPO). The primary focus at the onset of the PSC strategy execution was to confirm the completeness of the existing standardized work for each process. For example, were the steps of every process clearly written in the standardized work documents? Was the detail of the work visual and complete—including both written instructions and pictures of critical elements? Was the sequence of process elements correct? Were key points or descriptions included that would define the quality assurance elements of the process? Was the standardized work accessible to all team members? These are basic questions and really not unique to the PSC strategy, but nonetheless, we did find many nonconformities. Before continuing on to the next step, the standardized work was brought back to a base condition, and the methods for confirming the future adherence were reexamined. The reflection from this activity wasn't that we needed to change our approach to creating standardized work, but rather we learned a tough lesson about not following a good "Check" in our P–D–C–A cycle for confirming it. Improvement to the confirmation process became the main level-up point from this activity.

Next in the ABILITY step is PFMEA which stands for process failure mode and effects analysis. PFMEA is a standard process used throughout many industries to examine the input/output relationships found within a process. However, the steps we followed were slightly different than a conventional PFMEA. First, we did not perform a PFMEA for each and every manufacturing process (any Six Sigma guys still reading this are probably rolling their eyes right now). Instead, we grouped processes with similar inputs into buckets we called "main processes," and the PFMEA was performed only on these main processes. To perform a PFMEA on every manufacturing process in the paint and plastics shops would have taken months or perhaps even a year, but this approach was completed quickly and without compromising the integrity of the input/output assessment.

A second difference with our PFMEA process involved identifying and calculating not only Risk Factors (i.e., Severity × Likelihood of Occurrence × Likelihood of Detection) but also Control Factors (Process Training Level × Poka-yoke Reliability Factor × Inspection Reliability). Toyota typically uses these types of controls to manage process quality, so in effect, we were merely confirming the integrity of a system already in place. High risk factor failure modes found in processes with low control factors were prioritized for the most immediate countermeasure implementation and level up. If the risk factors could not be improved, then the next alternative was to improve the control factors. Ideally, the risk could be eliminated completely, but of course, this is rarely an alternative without significant expense. Control factors also generally add some operational cost, so countermeasure activity underwent close scrutiny to ensure the best, most holistic decisions were made. Decision-making matrices similar to the

Countermeasure Comparison Matrix shown in figure 8.4 were used to ensure all business conditions were considered.

PFMEAs will continue to be a work in progress. Failure modes are constantly being updated as new defects or failures occur in the processes, and new countermeasures are being implemented to lower each failure mode risk or improve the process controls. This has become a natural part of the P–D–C–A cycle for continuous improvement of the main processes. You may be wondering how new defects or failures could be occurring if the PFMEA process was done correctly. Well, the fact is that we missed some failure modes because we only knew what we knew. Despite our best efforts in our initial attempts to predict all of the failure modes, some outputs were missed due to the high complexity of the main processes. Fortunately, inspection gates internal to our processes were able to detect defects created by the gaps in our analysis and prevent them from flowing out to our customers.

The final ABILITY block substep is professional skill development. This is one of those processes that existed within Toyota prior to the PSC initiative, but the level of completeness varied all over the map. The concept of professional skill can best be described as the unique skills that go beyond the normal standardized work instructions. Sometimes referred to as "knack," these skills tend to be acquired over time through repetition versus knowledge that can be learned through information assimilation. The goal was to create standards for the knack skills so they could be taught and assessed prior to releasing team members to their process. In the past these skills would be acquired over time while team members produced customer's vehicles.

Once knack skill standards and training curriculum had been developed, the final instruction for these skills took place in what we referred to as main process "schools." Just as team members were all trained to perform the standardized work elements for their processes, they were now also required to attend and successfully complete the school for their main process. Successful completion involved both a written skill comprehension test and a hands-on assessment.

Once each of the ABILITY elements had been completed, the next step was to continue on to the AUTHORITY block—TPS Skill Enhancement and Training.

Both of these items are also quite common in Toyota operations, but of all the steps in this PSC strategy, AUTHORITY improvement was the one we most underestimated. We knew that our TPS skill was not where it needed to be, but we significantly misjudged the current level of TPS understanding and application—both within management and with the team members.

All Toyota team members received basic, introductory TPS theory training when they were hired, but we wrongly assumed that our employees were also practicing good TPS application in their daily work. The production areas appeared to be following TPS guidelines, but the comprehension element was almost totally missing. People were going through the motions and copying what they had seen done in the past, but by and large, they could not apply the logic of why they were doing what they were doing. TPS had become institutionalized right under our very noses.

So the focal point of the TPS training was to reeducate the "why" of Toyota manufacturing. When we started discussing this within small groups, we discovered many different levels of understanding. The purpose of building AUTHORITY is to define roles and responsibilities and set expectations, but how could this be achieved when everyone had a different understanding of why they're performing certain elements of their work? The answer of course is that it cannot. The "grassroots" TPS training was considered an enhancement to what the team members already knew. We didn't start from scratch. They already recognized many of the concepts and the vocabulary, but we wanted to teach them how to apply these TPS skills in a practical way. The final confirmation of the TPS training was to have each team member perform an assessment of one of his processes—a mini-jishuken if you will. We asked them to use the TPS tools they'd been taught (*yamazumi*, walking charts, combination work tables, layouts and element times, etc.) to confirm the completeness of a process they already knew quite well. We would then not only use these assessments to judge the TPS comprehension and capability of the team member, but we would also use this information to level up any significant process issues he had identified.

Soft skill or management elements of TPS and the Toyota Way were also added here in the block two training. Specifically, we found that team members were not following jidoka and managing the andon to stop problems from moving between processes. As already discussed in the "TPS Basics" chapter, I feel that jidoka is not intuitive to most Western culture workers. There may be other reasons why this counterculture exists, but my observation has been that stopping processes and having downtime is not something that most team members want to do—at least not those working in an automotive assembly plant. Automotive work is hot, physically demanding, and most people just want to get done with work as quickly as possible. This translates into not stopping the line and mismanagement of the intended use for the andon.

Of course, the conflict here is that when you have a problem but don't stop the line, how is the problem actually handled? Here are a few possibilities:

1) Nothing is done—the problem just keeps moving down the line.
2) The team member works faster and, therefore, doesn't follow standardized work as the problem is being corrected.
3) Someone is called to fix the problem (most likely a team leader in Toyota's case), but there is no follow-up to understand why the problem occurred—the root cause if you will.

In many situations, the problem does get fixed but only at the expense of extra effort by team members who had nothing to do with creating the problem initially. There's really only one correct team member response when he identifies a problem—pull the andon. This is one practical way that TPS is used to highlight problems. The andon is the team member's first line of defense against passing defects, and it's his primary tool for registering problems with management. Stopping the line protects the team members from performing nonstandard work, work which raises the risk of unwanted consequences, such as creating additional defects or injuries.

It would have been impossible for us as a management team to continue down the path of deploying our PSC strategy using the 4As approach if we hadn't taken the time to retrain and reemphasize the significance of following these "soft skill" TPS guidelines. We depend on team members to follow these guidelines all the time—especially when they're not being directly watched. Setting the expectation to use the andon properly was a crucial step toward improving quality. Does this mean the expectation was missing before? Perhaps. My judgment was that there were multiple levels of management that knew firsthand that the andon was not being used properly, but for the sake of avoiding confrontation or not taking the time to coach a team member, the violation was overlooked. That being said, I didn't feel that we as management could just turn on a dime and all of a sudden start enforcing what we hadn't done a good job of enforcing previously. This would not have shown good leadership integrity. Instead, we restated the expectation for andon use at all levels and then we proceeded with the remainder of the 4As—a drawing a "new-line-in-the-sand" approach.

As with the first block ABILITY, all of the evaluations, system development, training, and assessments for block two AUTHORITY were completed prior to moving onto the third block—ALIGNMENT. Let's do a quick refresher again so as not to make any assumptions regarding what you've retained up to this point in the book. ALIGNMENT is all about bringing purpose to work. Our goal here was to continue to build on the skill, the roles, and the expectations that had already been taught to the team members and to now help them establish a "why" behind the work; specifically—why is quality important to Toyota, to me, to my team, and to all of Toyota's stakeholders?

Block three consists of two substeps; Shop Floor Management (SFM) and Primary Process Owner (PPO). Let's do another quick refresher—SFM can be summarized into three main activities:

1) Visual management and/or 4S
2) KPI measurement, visualization, and management
3) Change point management

In chapter 10, these three activities were covered in some detail, so I will not cover them again here. What I do want to emphasize, however, is the purpose for integrating SFM into process self-completion. The high-level purpose for SFM is to create conditions in gemba where anyone can assess the current performance level. Within PSC the focus is specifically on the team members—the people performing the processes. To guarantee built-in quality at each process, we as management wanted to ensure that each person knew exactly how his process was performing. Visual management, KPI measurement, and change point management are all tools that enable team members to engage in their work, to take pride in their accomplishments, and to stay connected with the other stakeholders in the company.

The primary refinement to SFM as related to this ALIGNMENT step was in the area of visualization and the overall engagement of the team members. We discovered many varying levels of understanding and engagement with the information found on their SFM boards. Much to our discontent, the information on these boards had become wallpaper—pretty graphs and visuals that were on display but not being used to manage. The purpose for this SFM substep was to retrain and reengage team members in their understanding of process results—particularly process results in the area of quality. Many team members had not considered how their quality at the process level contributed to the overall quality of the vehicle. This wasn't their fault. This was a problem with how we were managing and sharing information with our teams. In the past, we simply posted KPIs and other information on the SFM boards, assuming that team members understood our message and our direction. Some group leaders were meeting with their teams at the boards, but not consistently and not to the level that we needed to ensure good team member engagement.

This SFM step was still a work in progress when I left Toyota, but the image was that somehow we would need to dedicate more time and resources to review the SFM information with team members. Senior management would need to commit to making this time available to GLs so they in turn could keep team members updated on their Process KPI progress compared with company performance goals. As we discussed in chapter 10, most people want to know how they're performing. Without a basic understanding of performance, there can be no recognition of the need for correction on the part of the team members. Most importantly, if there's no connection of process results to company performance, the workers executing the process cannot achieve ALIGNMENT.

The second step of ALIGNMENT was PPO. PPO was a familiar process within Toyota, but its use was generally reserved for new model introduction timing. When a new vehicle was being developed, new standardized work would also be created. To streamline and simplify the training method for the new standardized work, each team member would be assigned a unique "primary process" which he would learn first. By ensuring that each person learned and could perform at least one, unique process, pilot vehicles could be built on the same production lines alongside the current mass-production vehicles. After the pilot stage was completed and the new model went into mass production, team members would be trained on a rotation of processes (the standard was a four-process rotation). At this point, the "primary process" had no significant meaning because four team members would know and rotate through each process.

Our idea for PSC was to bring the primary process activity of new model introductions into mass production by adding the element of "ownership." In other words, we wanted each team member to actually own one unique process out of the four that he rotated through (each team would have four PPOs—one for each process in their four job rotation). The PPO would have the responsibility for creating standardized work, maintaining the 4S, tracking KPIs, and initiating kaizen activities for the continuous improvement of his process. In the past, it was *implicit* that management wanted team members to engage in this type of activity, but there was no formal expectation set. As a result of not understanding the expectation, most people did not spend time making improvements or even sustaining the conditions of their processes. By the end of a production shift, most team members would complete some basic housekeeping tasks and then race out the door. They were exhausted and just wanted to go home.

Establishing PPO allowed management to set the formal *expectation* that team members would need to set aside time each week to perform these basic process sustainment and improvement activities. Of course, we intended to compensate them for this time, but they in turn would have to commit some of their "personal" or "home" time to making their process stronger. Our goal was to create this small sense of sacrifice in order to build ownership, engagement, and of course, ALIGNMENT with the greater purpose that Toyota was trying to achieve—to improve quality and regain our competitive advantage in the market.

The concept of improving quality sounded great, but it wasn't until we set the expectation of PPO that our team members could really understand what kind of commitment this was going to take from them. Up to this point, it was my belief that team members felt like improving quality was somehow a "management issue." Although they were building the vehicles (the core work), most of them did not connect their quality contribution with the overall quality success of the company. Was this simply denial on the part of team members or was management failing to engage them? In my opinion it was both, and this PSC strategy was targeted at improving both the capability of management and the engagement of team members.

The last comment on PPO is that most team members wanted to feel like they had a voice in their process and in their work. From their first day of employment at Toyota, they had been told that their ideas were important and their opinions were valued. Everyone from the top of the organization to the bottom believed in this philosophy, a philosophy that is essential to the Toyota Way culture. What got lost was the method by which this belief was practiced in the workplace. Over time, the mechanisms that allowed the process improvement cycle to occur broke down. Management began to think that they were smarter than the team members and they didn't need their input. Team members lost trust in management and became disengaged. The "honeymoon" of working for a new company wore off, and people became satisfied with having a job instead of being engaged by the idea of having a career. A sense of entitlement was created by management by allowing special teams to implement kaizens so individual team members wouldn't have to commit their "home" time to make improvements themselves. All of this happened slowly, and in the end, team members lost their voice, and management lost their ability to listen.

While establishing PPO, I found myself explaining to team members who were displeased by the expectation that they must improve their own process that they "could not have a voice in their process from the parking lot." In other words, if they had ideas and they wanted to be heard, they were going to have to roll up their sleeves and get involved personally. This was always the intent for process kaizen, and it's how kaizen is still done in Japan and in many other plants outside of the U.S. Management must commit to allowing team members to own their process. These cannot just be idle words. Employees must actually be given some latitude to improve their work, to initiate problem solving on their own, and to be creative. Team members on the other hand must be willing to commit themselves personally to making these things happen.

Here's an analogy for PPO—Consider the difference in owning versus renting a car. Most of us treat rental cars like dirt. After all, they're rental cars! But how do you value your own car? Do you have more incentive to treat it with care? If you say "no," then you probably aren't going to grasp my philosophy for PPO. On the other hand, if you answered "yes," then you understand the basic intention behind PPO.

The final application of PSC is the ACCOUNTABILITY or ACKNOWLEDGEMENT step of the 4As. This last block consists of only one element—Performance Management. Would it surprise you to know that although TMMK had a system for corrective action to address team member behavior issues, there was no process for addressing nonexempt performance issues? (I must add a few notes here to protect the credibility of the book by stating that TMMK's HR team would heavily dispute this statement. The approach supported by HR was to escalate poor performing team members down the same progression of corrective action used to correct behavior issues. I personally have a problem with this approach as I am a firm believer that performance and behavior should be managed separately. So from my perspective as the author, there was no performance management system for nonexempt workers.) Yes, the exempt workforce had a performance appraisal system based on a "pay for performance" model, but the nonexempt workforce had no performance management system. In staying true with the 4A methodology, I felt the final step to improving our quality would be the deployment of a system for hourly team member performance management.

One past hurdle that had prevented us from establishing a performance management system for team members was the lack of reliable information from which to manage. In the context of quality, we just didn't have a bona fide method to collect defect data and track quality issues back to specific people. (A side note regarding defects—the term *defect* used in the context of this section refers to a nonstandard quality condition with a vehicle. Toyota uses internal quality standards to judge the completeness of the finished vehicle. Anything outside of this standard is judged as a defect. Defects are detected internally using regular, permanent inspection processes. The defects discussed in this section do not refer to problems with customers' finished vehicles, but instead refer to defects found by these internal inspection processes.)

So step 1 was to create a reliable system for tracking defects back to specific occurrences and to specific people. To ensure that team members felt the data was trustworthy, we allowed them to collect and track it. Now we didn't allow them to collect and track their own data, but rather we chose team members from different areas in production to track and monitor each other. The trick was using "customer" team members to track and feed back information to "supplier" team members. A customer team member is defined as anyone whose process is downstream of another given process (i.e., they are customers because they receive the output from preceding processes).

Prior to implementing a performance management system, customer team members felt the burden of having to deal with defects that were being passed on to them. These defects would many times cause the customer downtime or at the very least some abnormality to their standardized work. Other than the occasional "hey you're sending us defects" and some generic tracking on the supplier's defect KPI board, there wasn't any real consequence for passing on defects. But why didn't the supplier team initiate some problem solving activities to prevent the defects? The answer is that they did work on problems, but the solutions never addressed individual team member performance. The problems could not be broken down to that level because the data to support this analysis simply didn't exist. The problems were therefore generally assumed to be a process or equipment-related issue versus a team-member-related issue. Please don't misinterpret what I'm saying here. There were plenty of material, machine, and method issues, but there were also man issues that were not being addressed.

As you can imagine, there was quite an incentive for the customer team members to start tracking defects back to the supplier areas. To ensure the data was reliable, we as management not only had to allow team members to collect the data themselves, but we also had to narrow the tracking to defects we could be certain beyond any doubt were in their control to either create or prevent. By this time, we had already completed the "main process" PFMEA's, and therefore, we had a pretty good understanding of which defects were created by "man" process inputs. As the customer team members were trained to track and collect defect data, we also trained them regarding the types of defects that were created solely by "man" inputs. (We referred to these defects as "team member controllable.") In the end, the team members supported this defect-tracking method because peers who they trusted were collecting the defect data, and they accepted the assignment of team member controllable defects because the PFMEA used to correlate defect input/out was already established and understood.

With the first step completed, we began to develop the final steps of the performance management system—feedback, setting expectations, countermeasure activity, and confirmation of results. The feedback system was pretty simple, because we already had established the use of KPI boards in all areas of each shop. To support performance management, we merely added team-member-defect tracking on these boards. Admittedly, this practice was initially met with some resistance, particularly by the HR team who felt people would be offended by displaying their performance data publicly. But most team members accepted the information being posted because our intentions were genuine and true to the Toyota Way culture—to use the data for improvement, not for humiliation.

As time passed, most team members did reduce their controllable defects and felt quite a sense of accomplishment. Actually, the only people who didn't support the display of their defects were the few folks who consistently performed poorly and didn't do much to improve. I found little empathy for these people. In fact, the entire reason for needing the performance management system in the first place was to address performance issues from habitual low performers who were impacting the whole team's results. After the data tracking and performance management systems stabilized and the easily resolved issues had been countermeasured, we could see that the majority of the chronic quality issues were actually coming from a very small percentage of the workers.

The setting of performance expectations came directly from the group leaders and was done one-on-one in a private setting. Each team member was given a target for the maximum number of controllable defects they could have based on achieving the shop's overall quality goals. In staying true to 4A thinking, our management team was careful to create an ALIGNMENT between company and individual objectives. Initially, the group leaders tracked the team members' performance over time to confirm trends in controllable defects. The focus wasn't on each defect created, but rather the emphasis was on understanding the broader patterns of performance over time. Of course, if a person showed some rapid decrease in performance, the group leader would meet with him immediately to understand what was happening. Since the system of defect tracking was new, the team members were also encouraged to monitor and challenge results if they felt the data were incorrect.

Because the individual targets were derived from company performance goals versus actual past results, we were very careful to assess the practicality of the targets we had set for the team members. This was done by not only comparing each team member's results to his own target but also by comparing his results to coworkers' results. My thinking was along the lines of "grading on a curve" or a normal distribution (the exact same concept discussed in chapter 12 and highlighted in figure 12.2). I expected to see performance results that varied based on a normal distribution, and ideally the target would be near the mean. Over time, however, if the target was not centered at the mean of the distribution, we would switch focus to those team members performing only at the very low end of the curve—say the lowest 10% of the performers. This was also a great opportunity for us to understand the practicality of our overall company target because the individual performance targets were derived from achievement of the company's goal.

Team members who received one-on-one coaching from the group leader were asked to develop an action plan to countermeasure their performance. They could utilize any resources at their disposal, but we wanted the plan to be created by the individual having the performance issue in order to build some ownership. The performance improvement idea was then reviewed with the group leaders and tracked to confirm results. Initially, the focus was on the process improvement. In other words, did the team member try to do what he said he was going to do to improve his quality? Was there commitment from the team member to follow through on the activity he had chosen? If so, it was believed that improved results would come over time. If he did not follow through with his improvement plan, the next stage of coaching from the group leader would probably involve some level of corrective action. You may be questioning the use of corrective action for a performance issue. After all, wasn't my concept to keep these two issues separate? Yes it was, but at the point where a team member failed to follow through on a commitment, in my mind this became a behavior versus a performance issue. Again, as long as the team member was putting forth genuine effort to improve, there was no corrective action. However, when he refused to take ownership for his performance we were forced to go down the corrective action path.

So how did we recognize good performers? Was there actually a process of ACKNOWLEDGEMENT? The plan for ACKNOWLEDGEMENT of high performers was to distinguish these team members publicly in some manner. Perhaps we would give them a pin or a patch for their uniform or display pictures of high-performing employees on a "Wall of Fame" somewhere in the shop. Whichever methods were chosen, we wanted to give recognition that was visible to everyone and above all things avoid giving financial rewards. I had already seen the entitlement that accompanied financial recognition in the past, and I wanted to avoid incentivizing team members who might perform only for their own benefit. The purpose of PSC was not to reward individual performance but rather to improve the overall quality of the completed vehicle. We wanted team members to understand how their individual contributions rolled up into the final product, but the emphasis was on the final product, not the individual work. Success was to be measured as a team; therefore, the best ACKNOWLEDGEMENT was when the entire facility was recognized for improved quality.

The final outcome of process self-completion is still unknown. Toyota is presently implementing different phases of PSC across the globe, and many of the approaches are still not standardized. As for what I tried to accomplish with my team at TMMK in the paint and plastics shops, I did feel that we were making progress to improve overall quality while focusing on each individual process. Our plan was used as a company benchmark on several occasions, and many other areas inside the plant were adopting our PSC philosophy (or components of it anyhow). The journey had just begun when I decided to leave Toyota, so I may never know the full outcome of these efforts. I've heard that some of the initiatives are going well and that others are not progressing or have even stopped. At any rate, the purpose of presenting this information in this text was not to showcase the results but rather to highlight a few significant points.

1) Toyota doesn't have this "manufacturing stuff" all figured out. Yes, even Toyota still struggles, and in my opinion the root of the struggles is with their management team. Toyota was built on "doing what is right," but that's not always easy to do when times are tough. Back in the 90s and the early part of this decade it was relatively easy to manage at Toyota. Products were in demand, the company was growing, and by and large, people were pretty satisfied with the company. When times got tough due to the economic downturn in 2008, people began to question why Toyota was slipping. Management couldn't run on autopilot anymore, and people were being asked to explain performance results. Their failure was in not following the roots of Toyota. The immediate focus from senior management was on results instead

of the processes. PSC was an attempt on TMC's part to bring focus back to the production process—the place where TPS and the Toyota Way concepts originated. Focusing on processes when results must improve quickly isn't easy, but this is how Toyota is expected to manage every day.

2) I am writing this book to capture the skills and knowledge that I have acquired over my career. When I left Toyota, I felt confident that others could gain value from my experiences. Many of those experiences came from Toyota, but others came from my own personal leadership development. As with most people, the majority of my significant personal development points were learned from the errors that I made. I would later grow from these mistakes and try to not repeat them in the future. I realize that every organization is different, and that's what makes the competition of our marketplace so exciting. We're all trying to question the status quo every day in order to achieve that competitive advantage needed to be successful, and, in some cases, just to survive. Your company may not want to implement everything that I've learned, and that's just fine. Only you can decide what might be of value for your organization. Again, my hope is that you too can learn from my experiences even if only a few of them are applicable to your business.

3) PSC is an example of going back to the manufacturing basics. I don't know if Toyota will come back as successful in the next decade as they have been in the last five, but I do know that they are not leaving their fate in the hands of others. Toyota still believes in the culture that began with Kiichiro Toyoda, and they also realize that perhaps that culture is partially responsible for putting them in the place they are today. Perhaps the biggest reflection from my PSC development is that Toyota (and I include myself in this) had become complacent with the "check" of the P–D–C–A process. Too many assumptions were being made without confirmation of what was actually happening in gemba. There are no shortcuts for TPS—even when you're Toyota!

CHAPTER 17

WHAT'S NEXT?

Throughout this book, I've shared my firsthand experiences of managing and leading an organization while applying TPS and the Toyota Way. For some of you, reading this may never amount to anything more than information stored away in your memory. There are, however, a few people who will be inspired to take action by learning more about these topics. This is ultimately my desire. Nothing gives me more satisfaction than seeing another person develop his professional skills, and this applies to anyone reading this text. I wrote this because I genuinely want to help those who are struggling to find ways to practically apply the principles of Lean and TPS. Reading this book or any book for that matter isn't a stand-alone solution, but I sincerely believe it is a step in the right direction. But what I want really doesn't matter. The question is, what do you want? What did you hope to gain from reading about my TPS and Toyota work experiences?

In chapter 12, I spoke about the downside of training when skills and information are not applied immediately. The same principles hold true for reading a book. What is the value of acquiring information if it merely gets stored away? Let's face it, in today's Internet society, there's no shortage of stored facts and information. What is missing, however, is the wisdom to use it. Despite how many facts a person might be storing in his memory, knowledge amounts to nothing without discernment and ultimately action. These days, businesses need leadership that is capable of taking information, applying wisdom to set a direction, and then ultimately tapping into the company's resources to turn strategies into deliberate activities.

Do gaps exist in your current management structure that prevent your business from achieving its full potential? Could applying some of what I've discussed make a difference in how your company performs? Regardless of your position within your organization, as a leader these are the very questions that I would expect you to be asking yourself. And as a lifelong learner, you must also continue to challenge your own world views and entertain the ideas and perspectives of others—even if you are currently achieving your goals. Remember, the first step in learning is admitting that you don't already know everything. The most difficult time to see opportunities and challenge the status quo is when you're successful. After all, why mess with something that's working? But this is actually the best time to consider new approaches. An environment of accomplishment builds confidence and high morale, both of which make fertile soil for challenging an organization to stretch beyond their current achievements.

If your company has already begun a Lean transformation and has experienced some success, I would suggest doing a sincere reflection on the concept of kaizen. You'll never be done with the work you've started. In the truest sense of TPS, there is always room for improvement. Tweaking and finessing the methods for transforming your business are a natural progression of the kaizen process. As a next step, I would encourage you to take some points from this book and fold them into the strategies you've already deployed. Continue challenging the current conditions of your business to reach beyond what you once thought was possible.

But can you see the opportunities for prolonged growth and financial reward? Chances are good that if you're immersed in a culture currently experiencing some benefits from a Lean transformation, you may not be able to spot the remaining opportunities without some assistance. This is true for several reasons:

1) You only know what you know. The introduction of new knowledge and skill into your organization will bring additional perspective to your kaizen opportunities. Learning from others is a form of yokoten, a proven method to realize quick, sustainable results.

2) The low-hanging fruit is gone. When starting a Lean transformation, the opportunities are abundant. Further identification of waste may require a more detailed understanding and application of the TPS tools.

3) You can't see the forest for the trees. You're simply blind to the waste because the current conditions have become normal. You've come so far since beginning the Lean transformation that the status quo of the current conditions isn't recognizable.

The performance of athletes illustrates this point perfectly. Even athletes at the very top of their game use coaches to gain alternate perspective on their mechanics and their methods. In 2004, Tiger Woods began working with a new coach even though he had already won eight major tournament titles. Since that time, Tiger has won six more majors despite going through several personal hardships. The fear of "messing with success" didn't stop Tiger Woods's desire to take his performance to the next level. To do so, he knew he would need some help from someone who could be objective and offer personal insight.

If, on the other hand, your business is currently struggling to be competitive or profitable, you may be feeling the pressure to transform operations. But where should you start? In the presence of numerous opportunities, one may tend to struggle finding the optimum strategy or even taking the first step. The best advice I have to offer came from a friend of mine. The other day, we were discussing this very scenario, and he said the right approach is to tackle the biggest problem first. Now, this may sound pretty simple, but in the context of applying TPS, I thought his answer was very insightful. My instincts kept pushing me toward some type of Lean solution, but he looked at this situation in a much more practical way. He began by asking the most fundamental of questions—how can I help you improve your business?

At the end of the day, the solution to your company's problems may not be TPS, but everyone can benefit from improved problem solving. This is where the tires hit the pavement and where tangible results can be realized. My buddy's approach was to tackle the biggest problem and then apply tools for visualizing the real opportunities while stepping through the problem solving process (chapter 8). Maybe implementing some of the TPS tools will be useful at this point, but deploying them initially just for the sake of initiating a Lean transformation is probably not beneficial. Here's the analogy: If a person walks into the dentist's office with a toothache, he doesn't want to get a lesson on oral hygiene; he wants someone to take care of his pain. The reality of the patient's pain is more important than proactive strategies. Once his condition has stabilized, the patient might be more open to listening to preventative measures.

This is the same practical approach that businesses should take when considering a Lean transformation. The first step is to stabilize your operations through good problem solving. Don't be misled into believing that by introducing a 4S system or some improved standardized work your business will become more profitable. Even learning formal kaizen techniques will not improve your operations if the other TPS tools aren't in place. Starting a transformation by applying the tools found in the foundation of the TPS house will take significant time and effort. In addition to this, you're going to need capable people to teach and lead your company through this type of activity. If your business is already struggling, chances are now is not the right time to begin a full-blown transformation.

It's like I said at the beginning of this book. TPS is nothing more than a set of tools—just like a hammer and a saw. Being able to use any individual tool doesn't qualify a person to be a carpenter. Would you hire a carpenter whose only skill is cutting boards with a saw? Of course you wouldn't. The objective of the carpenter isn't to use the tool but rather to build something. The tool is merely a means to another end. The same holds true to applying Lean tools and concepts. Knowing how to implement 4S alone will not make your business any better. Sure, things might look cleaner and more organized, but this isn't TPS, and it certainly won't impact your operations significantly. To get where I think you really want to go, you're going to need a comprehensive strategy which incorporates both the hardware and the software that Toyota has mastered over the past half century. Most importantly, you're going to need to create a corporate culture where people feel valued and problems are seen as opportunities.

So here I sit after months of tapping out words on this keyboard, and I find myself reflecting on that same conversation I had with my buddy while drinking a beer. Do I see my future as a Lean consultant? Isn't that partially what I've done by writing this book? Perhaps, but I'd like to think of myself as more of a coach than a consultant. Maybe it's semantics, but I want to believe that the approach of a coach is a little different. Coaches improve upon the skill that someone already has, but they don't play the game for him. Consultants, on the other hand, might be perfectly content with doing the work by themselves. How does this approach strengthen your organization? What happens with the skill once the consultant leaves?

If I'm the dentist in the analogy of the guy with the toothache, the question I have to ask is when should I transition from treating the pain to addressing the process? Sure, I could make a living by filling people's teeth all day long, but how much satisfaction is there in that? Who knows, if there's enough interest in the material presented in this book, I just might publish a "cookbook" detailing the steps I've taken to implement many of these strategies and concepts. This is after all what most people seem to want—"Tell me less about what I should be doing and show me how to do it."

In closing, I'd like to leave you with these final thoughts. I've spent a lot of time talking about Toyota in this book, and I may have given you the impression that they have Lean management all figured out. Nothing could be further from the truth. From what I've seen, however, they are still one of the very best when it comes to applying TPS principles and sustaining results. Toyota is also committed to continuous improvement. They may get off course every now and then, but they've stayed pretty true to their culture and to their core beliefs. Their approach can help any business (not just a manufacturing business), but only when it is applied properly. The bigger operational impact to Toyota's results comes from their ability to effectively solve problems. These skills are separate from TPS, but they too can have a profound impact on any business. Let's face it, who couldn't benefit from better problem solving?

Like any process, both TPS and problem solving can be learned, given the right approach and instructor. If you're tired of trying the same things only to achieve the same results over and over, perhaps it's time for you to get a coach. You must already have some of the right tools or you would have never made it this far reading my book. Take the next step to transform yourself and your business. You won't regret your efforts.

GLOSSARY

4S/visual management—One of the TPS foundation elements. The 4S's stand for sort, straighten, sweep, and standardize. 4S is a system of workplace management used to help highlight waste in a process.

Andon—A system used by the operator of a process to stop the progress of that process when abnormality is detected. The andon is also used by the operator as a means of registering a problem with management.

CPM—An acronym for change point management; the management of any condition that triggers a change in a process.

Child plant—The name used in reference to a new plant located outside of Japan which is being supported by a mother plant.

Combination work table—A tool used to organize and display all the work elements of a process for the purpose of analyzing the process for waste.

Fishbone diagram—A problem solving tool used to organize brainstorming and eventually isolate the root cause of a problem. The Fishbone Diagram gets its name because visually the diagram resembles the skeleton of a fish.

GL—A Toyota acronym for a group leader. This is the first level of supervision and management in the organization and the entry level for exempt employees.

Gemba—The place where work occurs.

Genchi genbutsu—A Toyota term loosely translated "go and see"—meaning to go to gemba and confirm a work condition for yourself.

Heijunka—The leveling or smoothing of production to reduce process fluctuations.

Hoshin—A type business plan used by Toyota. They are generally created to set strategic direction for periods of one or five years.

JIT—A Toyota acronym for just in time. This philosophy teaches that all material and products should move at the correct time (based on a pull system), in the correct quantity (ideally one-piece flow).

Jishuken—The process used by Toyota to develop TPS skills by studying and improving actual work conditions in gemba. Loosely translated, jishuken means "self-study."

Jidoka—Preventing a defect from passing to the next processes.

KPI—An acronym for key performance indicator. KPIs are used to measure process performance and company results.

Kaizen—Continuous improvement.

Kanban—Literally translated as "signboard" or "graphic," Toyota uses this word to describe a signal used to replenish inventory.

Lean—A term used frequently outside of Toyota to refer to TPS or other systems that target operational cost reduction.

Mother plant—The reference to a Japanese plant supporting a new, transplant facility. The mother plant will typically support the transplant (or child plant) indefinitely.

NUMMI—An acronym for New United Motor Manufacturing Inc. This was Toyota's first manufacturing joint venture with General Motors located in Fremont, California. The plant operated between 1984 and 2010 and is best known for manufacturing the Toyota Corolla and the Toyota Tacoma.

OJD—A Toyota acronym for on-the-job development. This is a process used by Toyota to develop deeper levels of skill. This process involves one-on-one coaching and mentorship, generally between a supervisor and a subordinate.

Organizational equilibrium—A term coined by the author to refer to all of the circumstances and conditions that exist currently within an organization (for example: policies, procedures, cultural norms, the physical environment, individual employees and their unique behaviors, etc.).

PFMEA—An acronym for process failure mode and effects analysis. The PFMEA is a somewhat common process used throughout industry to analyze and ultimately improve or eliminate the risk factors associated with any given process.

PKA—An acronym for practical kaizen activity. PKA is often used synonymously outside of Toyota to refer to any kaizen activity.

PSC—An acronym for process self-completion. PSC is a management strategy used to ensure that each process can be confirmed for accuracy and completion by the operator performing the work.

Poka-yoke—A device, system, or process characteristic which assists the operator to not pass a defect or a mistake out of his process.

SFM—An acronym for shop floor management. SFM refers to the methods or processes used to ensure that the core work is being managed systematically. The purpose of SFM is to engage the workers by making process conditions visual and easy to understand.

SPC—An acronym for statistical process control. SPC is a reference to the use of statistical methods to monitor and control the inputs and outputs of a process.

Six Sigma—A business management strategy used throughout industry for the purpose of minimizing variation in a process.

Stakeholder—Anyone who relies on your business's success.

Standardized work—The written documentation detailing the elements of work performed in a process.

TL—A Toyota acronym for a team leader. A team leader is a nonexempt employee and therefore not a member of management. Team leaders are trained to support operations by addressing abnormal conditions experienced by team members performing standardized work. In some industries, team leaders may also be referred to as utility or relief personnel.

TM—A Toyota acronym for a team member. A team member is the nonexempt employee who performs the manufacturing processes. In some industries, team members may also be referred to as operators or associates.

TMC—An acronym for Toyota Motor Corporation. This is the name given to the corporate operations of Toyota located in Toyota City and Nagoya, Japan.

TMMI—An acronym for Toyota Motor Manufacturing, Indiana. The Toyota vehicle assembly plant located in Princeton, Indiana, which produces Sequoia, Highlander, and Sienna. This is also the startup facility where I began working at Toyota in 1997. I left TMMI in 2007.

TMMK—An acronym for Toyota Motor Manufacturing, Kentucky. The Toyota vehicle assembly plant located in Georgetown, Kentucky, which produces Camry, Avalon, and Venza. I transferred to this facility from 2007 to 2011.

TPS—A Toyota acronym for Toyota Production System. This is a system or a group of tools which Toyota has developed for the purpose of finding waste in a process.

Takt time—The required pace for manufacturing that matches the customers' demand for the products being made.

Toyota Way—The defining values of Toyota.

Transplant—Any Toyota facility located outside of Japan.

WIP—An acronym for work in process. WIP is a term used to describe partially completed inventory stored between manufacturing processes.

Walking chart—A visual TPS tool used to outline the path a team member physically walks while performing his standardized work.

Yamazumi—A TPS tool used to visualize the cumulative work element times that make up a process's total cycle time.

Yokoten—A Toyota term meaning to implement a proven solution or countermeasure somewhere else. Ideally the countermeasure is improved from the original solution.

Made in the USA
Lexington, KY
16 May 2012